"This student's guide  ry
skill. Writing in a strai   up
her discussion with s}   :ia
Dutcher-Walls lays out a sensible reading plan for any who wish to
take the Bible seriously in all its aspects: literary, historical, and theological. Her numerous examples from ancient Near Eastern sources
locate the Bible in its world, and her frequent modern illustrations
help readers connect. Useful sidebars and stimulating study questions enhance the pedagogical attractiveness of the volume. Both
author and publisher are to be congratulated on a fine book that
should gain a wide readership."

—**V. Philips Long**, Regent College, Vancouver

"*Reading the Historical Books* provides an excellent supplementary
text on methodology for anyone teaching the Former Prophets.
Dutcher-Walls builds on the reading experience of students to explore such critical topics as social context, narrative technique, and
theology that are part of the fabric of ancient history writing. Summary questions for reflection guide students through the reading
process. Only after students have become familiar with the texts
through firsthand reading does the volume conclude with a broad
discussion of ancient historiography and how it has shaped the
writing of Israel's history in the Former Prophets."

—**Tom Dozeman**, United Theological Seminary

"Professor Dutcher-Walls has given us an excellent treatment of
the principles of history writing that guided the historians of this
corpus of biblical literature. A judicious examination of texts from
ancient Near Eastern literature reveals that these same principles
may be found in that larger body of texts as well. Further, she has
demonstrated ably that an awareness by the contemporary reader
of how these ancient historians told their stories will greatly assist
one in engaging the biblical text. Numerous examples from modern
media such as family histories, film, and Facebook show that even
yet we tell our own stories, *mutatis mutandis*, in very similar ways
to the ancient historiographers. I am happy to recommend *Reading
the Historical Books*."

—**Victor P. Hamilton**, Asbury University

READING THE HISTORICAL BOOKS

A STUDENT'S GUIDE TO ENGAGING THE BIBLICAL TEXT

PATRICIA DUTCHER-WALLS

Baker Academic
a division of Baker Publishing Group
Grand Rapids, Michigan

© 2014 by Patricia Dutcher-Walls

Published by Baker Academic
a division of Baker Publishing Group
P.O. Box 6287, Grand Rapids, MI 49516-6287
www.bakeracademic.com

Printed in the United States of America

Library of Congress Cataloging-in-Publication Data is on file at the Library of Congress, Washington, DC.

ISBN 978-0-8010-4865-4

14 15 16 17 18 19 20   7 6 5 4 3 2 1

To my students over the years,
for their good questions and keen insights.
You always wanted to know
what *my* interpretive principles were,
since I worked you so hard to figure out your own.
Well, here are some of them.

Contents

Acknowledgments

My sincerest thanks to those who helped this book come to fruition. First, I am thankful to Steven McKenzie for suggesting the idea both to Baker Academic and to me. The receptive editor at Baker Academic, Jim Kinney, and his whole team were a wonderful group with whom to work. The project depended on a sabbatical during which a large portion of the manuscript was written, so my gratitude goes to the Vancouver School of Theology. I am very appreciative of the Sorrento Retreat and Conference Centre, where I enjoyed an "introvert's heaven" for one month of writing. My appreciation goes also to colleagues in various sections of the Society of Biblical Literature for stimulating discussions over the years about all the topics this book covers. My special thanks to Ms. Margaret Miller and Ms. Maryann Amor, proofreaders and editors extraordinaire, for their careful work with the manuscript. Finally, to my husband, Tim, who, besides having superb pastoral skills, cooks a great dinner for his long-commuting wife.

Abbreviations

BCE	before the Common Era
cf.	compare
chap(s).	chapter(s)
Chron.	Chronicles
Deut.	Deuteronomy
Dtr	Deuteronomist
ed.	editor, edition
et al.	*et alii*, and others
Exod.	Exodus
Josh.	Joshua
Judg.	Judges
Lev.	Leviticus
Neh.	Nehemiah
Sam.	Samuel
trans.	translator
vol(s).	volume(s)

Introduction

Imagine that you are poking around an attic full of stuff at your grandmother's house, helping clean out several decades' worth of family belongings. You discover a very old book, handwritten, and after examining it further, find that it is a family history. The book seems to be like a diary, and it contains an account of some of your ancestors, several generations back. The early pages are written in a foreign language, and when it switches to English it is written in very simple sentences but in beautiful handwriting. A few very old photographs are stuck between the pages. You do not recognize anyone in the pictures, the clothes seem funny and very old-fashioned, and there is a car in one that looks like something in a museum. You abandon your dusty work in the attic and take the book to your grandmother. She smiles and handles the book almost reverently as she says it is the family story written by her great-grandfather to record his family's adventures in moving from the old country. The last part of the book is from her mother, adding stories that are more recent. From the dates on some of the early pages you realize that the book is over 150 years old. Your grandmother suggests that you would enjoy reading the book, and with that encouragement to abandon the task in the attic, you spend a fascinating afternoon reading an old history.

You quickly realize that this writing is not like anything you usually read. It is certainly not like the text messages and tweets you zip off to your friends all day, or like the newspapers your parents read at the breakfast table. It is also not like most of the websites and blogs you cruise around on looking for answers to homework questions. It is written like a story, but it also contains lots of references to dates and places, a couple of which you have heard of. It is pretty much in chronological order and seems to be careful about recording events that happened to your ancestors along their journeys. In a few cases, the events seem to have a background of world affairs that you have heard about—the First World War and the Depression. In some ways it seems a little like the textbooks you read in your high school history classes. However, you realize there are some occurrences that seem very weird to you, and the people talked about have some experiences that you do not understand at all. Sometimes there are comments expressing a strong opinion about an event or about someone else in the family. Throughout the book there is a sense of pride and satisfaction in the hard work and accomplishments of the family. You end your afternoon fascinated and a bit confused about what you have read. You seem to have entered a world different from your own even though some of it seems familiar.

Just what are you reading? What is this document? Why is it written this way? What else do you need to know to understand it well? If you talked with your grandmother, would she be able to explain some things you do not understand? Maybe you would need a map to figure out some of the places named, and a better understanding of the events of the time period to which the writing refers. You might need a bit of a tour guide to give you some background about the book.

This imaginary scene highlights some of the issues and curiosities that also happen when we read the Bible. In particular, when we read the parts of the Old Testament that can be called the historical books, we are looking at writing that is not too far removed from the family history of this little scene. If you had never heard of the

Bible and someone handed you a copy, the experience of reading a book like 1 Kings or Ezra would be similar to that in our imaginary scene. The historical books certainly seem to record a story about events, places, and people, more or less in chronological order. There seems to be a reverence for what is recorded, and the writing has some definite opinions about religious realities. And yet, there are still good questions about just what it is that you are reading. What is this document? Why is it written this way? What else do you need to know to understand it well? If you talked with someone who knows about the world of the Bible, would that person be able to explain some things you do not understand? Maybe you would need a map to figure out some of the places named, and a better understanding of the events of the time period to which the writing refers. In the briefest way of putting it, this book hopes to be a tour guide that can give you some background about the historical books of the Old Testament. Later in the book we will come back to imaginative scenes like the one above to help illustrate more about the Bible.

The focus of our study is this: How do we read the historical books in the Old Testament well? What do we need to know about this part of Scripture in order to appreciate the beauty and meanings of the text? This small volume will introduce you to aspects of the genre of history writing in the Old Testament in order to make your further reading and study of Scripture more informed and sensitive. We will concentrate on books in the Old Testament that can be termed historical: Joshua, Judges, 1 and 2 Samuel, 1 and 2 Kings, 1 and 2 Chronicles, Ezra, and Nehemiah. (Joshua to 2 Kings as a unit is called the Deuteronomistic History because these six books have similarities in outlook and theology to the book of Deuteronomy.) We will explore both the artistry and form of the text and the world behind the text that shaped the writing of these important parts of Scripture.

The Old Testament is an ancient document that, at least initially, needs to be taken on its own terms by modern readers seeking a faithful and informed understanding. Modern assumptions about how one reads a historical account, a novel, a text message, or a website may not bring the best awareness and assumptions for reading a text that is more than two thousand years old. The goal of this volume is to sensitize readers of the historical books in the Bible to the forms, writing styles, assumptions, and background that an ancient audience might have taken for granted when reading or hearing a passage of Scripture but that might be invisible to a modern audience.

The basic approach of the volume is to *take the text of Scripture seriously* as the focus of attention. All the insights helpful for understanding the genre of history writing will begin with the text as you might read it, using a good English translation. Any comments made about the content of a passage or the background of the text will grow out of qualities and phenomena that a reader of Scripture might observe. In this sense, nothing will be imposed on the text that a careful reader might not have already been able to discern, although it is my hope that the guidance of this volume will help you as a reader to be more sensitive to particular qualities of biblical writing. This inductive approach will build on your own observations, while introducing topics that will enhance and deepen your understanding.

This volume will not replace a good standard introduction to the Old Testament. Rather, this book is designed to complement or help one prepare for a more in-depth study of the historical books. In the first chapter, the basic historical background of the Old Testament will be given to clarify the setting of the historical texts. However, because of the brief format of this volume, no attempt will be made to cover all the topics of an introductory textbook. Methods such as text, source, form, and redaction criticism are helpful for understanding aspects of a text and ideas about how Scripture came to be, but this book will not focus on them directly. This means that the book assumes that you will read elsewhere about standard introductory questions regarding setting, authorship, dating of the books, sources, canon, and so on. Also, because of the brief format of the volume, no attempt will be made to cover the whole content of the biblical historical books themselves, although you will find numerous examples of passages drawn from these historical books.

I am deeply aware that readers of the volume have a number of different understandings about the inspiration of Scripture, some closely held and others perhaps unexamined. You may have grown up attending church and believing in God's direct inspiration of the Bible. Other readers may have never read the Bible at all and have no particular opinion as to whether it is inspired. No matter what stance a reader brings, the volume will assume that learning to take the text of Scripture seriously will provide insights about how to read the text better, and thus, how better to engage the text for all other purposes or commitments. The book also does not take a particular stand on the extent to which the events recorded in the biblical books happened the way they are described. Rather, our focus is on how the texts themselves remembered and recorded an account of the past that was important for the communities and people who wrote the historical books.

Outline of the Book

The first chapter takes a look at how the story conveyed in the historical books reveals the context out of which it emerged. The biblical story reflects the time, setting, and social world of its era. The social institutions that interact with the events reported, the characters that populate the stories, the backgrounds of villages, cities, and states that are the landscape—all of these are inherent in the text and reflect the context of the biblical books. This is a world far different from that of modern readers. For example, you may not have a good sense of the foreign nations that bordered ancient Israel, or of the presence of extended families in peasant societies, or of elite royal houses that governed those societies. Yet the geographical location, family dynamics, and royal institutions are the setting of the Bible. Seeing how this context appears in the biblical books and understanding more of this ancient world will help you comprehend the writing in the biblical books in more depth. To make sure that the basic story line of the historical books is familiar, this chapter also weaves the story told by the people of ancient Israel into the review of the context. This chapter combines approaches from fields including sociology, anthropology, geography, economics, archaeology, and history to discover the settings that are the background of the history writing in the Bible. The resulting reading skills will allow you to see a larger world in and behind the texts.

The second chapter takes the text of the historical books seriously by demonstrating how they work as stories. History writing in the Old Testament is almost always cast as a story, with typical elements of storytelling at work, such as plot, characterization, time sequencing, and point of view. Starting with excerpts from the historical books that illustrate typical facets of narrative art, this chapter highlights the kinds of storytelling techniques used by the ancient writers to shape the narratives they told. Using narrative analysis well established by biblical scholars, this chapter will help you see how a passage "works" as story. Modern assumptions about reading short stories or novels do not always generate sensitive readings of biblical narratives. For example, characterization in a modern novel is often quite full and descriptive, giving detail of a character's physical presence and inner thought life that makes the character fairly transparent to the reader. However, biblical characterization often functions through less direct means, rarely giving physical descriptions and even more rarely letting the reader "inside" the thoughts of the characters. Rather, characterization in biblical stories creates a sense of the character through descriptions of the character's actions, inclusion of sometimes extended dialogue, and indirect description by other characters. Being aware of this and other typical techniques in ancient storytelling will increase your ability to read the text well.

If you have read some of the Bible, you may have already observed that there seem to be particular points of view expressed in the accounts. The texts seem to dwell on religious ideas and sometimes express strong theological opinions, ideas that are shaped to be persuasive for the audience of the texts. The third chapter examines the principal ways that Old Testament passages convey the concepts and theology inherent in its writing. For example, such passages can persuade an audience about how bad a particular king was through direct evaluation ("the king did evil"), using commentary on a particular event or the actions of a particular character. In other cases, the interests of the text are carried by less obvious techniques by which the text draws your attention to certain ideas or events and omits or downplays other ideas and events. Such techniques include repetition of exact or similar phrases, which is one important way that ancient rhetoric worked. However, you have probably been taught in English classes to avoid repetition, and so you may be tempted to ignore or dismiss this aspect of the text. Being able to see the interests of an ancient text will help you to appreciate Scripture as something more than a seemingly objective "news report." Scripture is a highly shaped, convincing theological document that "works" as persuasive writing to convey the thought world of the text.

The final two chapters of the book look directly at how history was written in the biblical historical books. As theologically shaped stories, these ancient books are also evidently relating history—that is, they are telling a story about the past. These two chapters start from the assumption that the historical books recounted stories about events, people, and places of their own eras with seriousness and respect in order to bring out the meaning of history for their ancient audiences. However, ancient history writers did not always work in the way that history writers do in the present time. For example, modern conventions require history writers to refer to a wide variety of sources, to be more or less balanced in their approach, and to assume logical tenets (like observable cause and effect). These assumptions were not necessarily part of how ancient history was written. Ancient history writers had their own conventions about how to convey the past. We will discover the characteristics of how biblical history writers worked through examining how their texts express the story of the past. We will further explore the methods of ancient history writing by examining many examples of historical writings from other ancient societies. While the historical writings in the Bible focused, of course, on the history of God's people as the writers understood and conveyed it, the types of historical conventions they used can be helpfully compared with other ancient historical writings.

A brief concluding chapter pulls together the observations we have made about history writing as it appears in the biblical historical books. You will see in summary form the principal characteristics that mark this type of writing, and you will be able to begin to pick out for yourself the qualities that make biblical historical writing lively and meaningful. With the sensitivities you will have gained about how such writing conveyed its account of the past, you will be able to read with greater interest and knowledge. And you will see that biblical historical books are a lot more interesting than you might have thought; they are not all sleep-inducing lists of who begat whom. In their own right and in their own ways, they communicate important information, ideas, and messages about the past through historical storytelling.

Discussion Questions

1. Can you remember hearing stories or reading memoirs from your parents or grandparents about your family's history? What aspects of these stories struck you as odd or different from your life today? What did these stories or memories tell you about your family's history and identity?

2. What familiarity do you have with the Bible and the Old Testament? Survey your friends. How many seem to know the Bible well? How many seem not to be familiar with it?

3. While this book holds that the writers of the Old Testament understood in various ways that God was revealed and closely involved in their lives and history, modern readers will have a wide variety of opinions about this. What do you and each of your friends think was the role of divine revelation in the writing of the Bible?

1

Discovering the Context
of the Text

Writing about the past includes conveying a sense of the background behind the events being recorded. There is always a context for events, and that context provides the setting for what transpired—everything from the physical environment and the political and economic conditions at the time to the personal and social relationships that affected the events. Any event interacts with its context, and different contexts may create very different outcomes for similar events. If you have ever lived through an earthquake, you know that a highway built on bedrock will likely survive better than one built on landfill—same event, very distinctive outcomes. Or if two nations hold elections, one nation a democracy and one a totalitarian state, the elections will likely have very different outcomes in terms of political participation. To understand what happened in order to write intelligently about the two elections, you would have to know something about the particular circumstances of each election, like the political systems and each nation's history of electoral policies. Context makes a difference in the events of the past.

For example, if you received this text message from a friend whom you know pretty well, you would be able to decipher it easily:

> ahh man it was weird lol. cover was 20 bucks but yolo i guess
> so we went for it. saw jess there too, though she said not to
> tell you. i hope you're not mad, man. ended up dancing with
> robin hood and the wizard of oz people haha. so random.
> got home at like 2 i think? my mom and dad are choked,
> especially after last weekend

Since you know where your friend likes to hang out, you would not need an explanation about the locale to which he was referring. You would know that "Jess" was his former girlfriend, and that "Robin Hood" and the "Wizard of Oz" were costumed friends from a recent Halloween party. You would also know why it was so crucial that he be home on time for a curfew.[1] Also, if you are used to text messaging, you do not need to have the language itself translated. But imagine if your grandparents saw the text message—they would not only need the language to be translated into something they would recognize as English but would also need the background to be explained. For someone who does not know these things, understanding the context of the message is crucial for understanding its meaning. Context makes a difference in the events of the past and in writing about the past.

But let's go back to our opening statement: "Writing about the past includes conveying a sense of the background behind the events being recorded." This statement indicates another important aspect of "context": not only the background of the events themselves but the background of the writing about those events must be considered. People recording the past also have a context, an

---

1. My thanks to my son, Wesley Dutcher-Walls, for creating this text message for me. Translation: Ahh, man, it was weird. LOL [Laugh out loud]. The cover [entrance fee for the club] was twenty bucks, but YOLO [you only live once], I guess, so we went for it. I saw Jess there too, though she said not to tell you. I hope you're not mad, man. I ended up dancing with Robin Hood and the Wizard of Oz people. Ha, ha. It was so random [weird, unexpected]. I got home at, like, two, I think? My mom and dad are choked [very angry], especially after last weekend.

environment, a set of political, economic, and social circumstances that affect how they write about the past. If a historian is writing about contemporary and local events, then the contexts of the events and the writing are similar. However, historians may write about events in another part of the world or in a time period removed from their own. If so, then they have to be aware that their context is very different and their own awareness and assumptions about things may be distinct from the context they are writing about. The historians would need to take care to try to understand and re-create the context of the events in their own setting in order to give a good account.

Let's go back to the opening statement one more time: "Writing about the past includes conveying a sense of the background behind the events being recorded." There is actually a third context that eventually impacts a historical document—that of the *reader* of the account of the past. The reader may be in an environment or setting very different from that of either the original events or the written account. For example, you may have in your family's records an account by your great-grandmother of the story of her grandmother emigrating from another part of the world over 150 years ago. The events of the original time took place in the mid-1800s, perhaps in a time of great famine and hardship in your family's country of origin. The original characters in the story knew well the environment of the country of origin because they had lived there all their lives. But when your great-grandmother recounted the story maybe eighty years ago, she was living in the new country and did not know the old country at all. She had to rely on recounting the story as well as she could, trying to explain some of the traditions of the old country as they had been handed down for her new context. Now, when you read this account, you are living in still another context—one much different from either the original events of the emigration or the recounting of those events by your great-grandmother. You may need a family member to translate some of the words being used in the account or to explain some of the practices about century-old clothing or food or social expectations. Context makes a difference

in the events of the past, in writing about the past, and in reading
an account of the past.

Reading an Ancient Account of the Past

When we as twenty-first-century readers in the developed world
approach the historical books of the Old Testament, we are reading
a series of documents that were written over two thousand years
ago in a time and place very different from our own. The context
of the Bible is different in many ways from our context. Most of us
do not live in settings where travel is by donkey, where kings rule
exclusively by their own power, where communication is limited to
hand-carried messages, or where the planting of crops is done by
hand. However, the differences are not so drastic between the context
of the events recounted in the historical books and the context of
the writers of those books. The writers were living largely in the
same type of social structures and environmental, geographical, and
political settings as the account of the past they were writing, even
if some centuries had elapsed between certain of the events and the
writing and later editing of the accounts. The issue for us as readers
is to learn about the contexts of the biblical accounts of the past,
which for the ancient writers did not need explanation or definition.

A very general approach locates the context of the events and the
writing of the biblical historical books to a time period of roughly
one thousand years, from about 1300 BCE to about 300 BCE. The
location is what we call the ancient Near East, which runs from
Egypt in northern Africa through the eastern seaboard of the Mediterranean Sea, eastward through the vast valley of the Tigris and
Euphrates Rivers in ancient Mesopotamia (modern Iraq and Iran),
and westward through modern Turkey and Greece. Most of the
political states of that time were monarchies, each tightly controlled
by a dynastic family, or by competing dynastic families. Sometimes
a particularly powerful state acquired enough territory by conquest
or treaty to become an empire, reaping extra economic surplus but
needing military and economic controls over the larger territory.

Ancient economies were largely based on agriculture, with other economic resources located in trade, mining, herding, and fisheries, as well as limited skilled labor in jobs like metal and stone crafting. Much of a state's economic structure was controlled by the monarchy. Relationships among states involved both trade by treaty and outright conflict in wars of aggression that could bring additional resources and income. Roads were key structures within and especially among states. A road functioned as a pathway for trade and communication and for armies bent on conquest. Social structures were generally highly stratified, so that there was a large gap between a small number in the richest classes, usually the royal house and its officials, and the majority of the population in the poorest classes, usually peasant farmers. Political and religious realities and institutions were highly integrated—politics involved religion, and religion undergirded politics.

In what follows, we will look at some of the most important aspects of the context of the historical books of the Old Testament. To create this picture of the ancient world, fields of knowledge such as sociology, anthropology, geography, economics, archaeology, and history are combined. Such a social-world approach tries to understand patterns and relationships among social actors—from the macrolevel, like states and empires, to the microlevel, like families and towns. Rather than concentrating on individual events and actions of a particular person, such as a king, social-world studies look at how kings as a type of social actor characteristically behave, or how agrarian states usually order their national institutions. What emerges in such a social-world portrait is a description of typical relationships among social structures and social actors, which can give a good sense of the context for particular events and actions.[2]

2. Sociological studies about ancient Israel and Judah include Volkmar Fritz, *The City in Ancient Israel* (Sheffield: Sheffield Academic Press, 1995); Paula McNutt, *Reconstructing the Society of Ancient Israel*, Library of Ancient Israel (Louisville: Westminster John Knox, 1999); Philip J. King and Lawrence E. Stager, *Life in Biblical Israel*, Library of Ancient Israel (Louisville: Westminster John Knox, 2001); Charles E. Carter and Carol L. Meyers, eds., *Community, Identity, and Ideology: Social Science Approaches to the Hebrew Bible*, Sources for Biblical and Theological Studies 6 (Winona Lake, IN: Eisenbrauns, 1996); David J. Chalcraft, ed., *Social-Scientific Old*

An example of how social-world studies work to describe patterns rather than individual data comes from a college textbook that you may have read. For the tenth edition of *Human Societies: An Introduction to Macrosociology*, the cover illustration is a picture of Europe and Africa from space at night, showing the lights of cities. The blurb about the cover illustration in the book states, "The Cover, 'Global City Lights,' is an image created by Craig Mayhew and Robert Simmon of the National Aeronautics and Space Administration Goddard Space Flight Center, from Defense Meteorological Satellite Program data. The relative brightness and clustering of the lights indicate the degree of urbanization."[3] The life going on for individuals within the many cities pictured is probably quite fascinating, but one main interest of the sociologist is the degree of urbanization.

In doing our study of the context of the Old Testament we will start from the texts themselves. What do the texts reveal as the background of their writing? What realities, knowledge, and environments were parts of the unspoken background that the writers could take for granted because this setting was so similar to the one they also knew? What does the social world context of the historical books look like from a viewpoint inside these accounts of the past? As we do this text-based survey of the contexts of the historical books, we will also provide an overview of the flow of the biblical story as the texts themselves portray it, without making any particular commitments to whether events actually happened exactly as they are described. As we noted in the introduction, our job is not to write a history of ancient Israel but to explore how the biblical historical books work as history writing. So this overview is designed to give you a summary of the Old Testament's own account of its past. Also, as you go through this overview, note

---

Testament Criticism: A Sheffield Reader (Sheffield: Sheffield Academic Press, 1997); and J. David Schloen, *The House of the Father as Fact and Symbol: Patrimonialism in Ugarit and the Ancient Near East*, Studies in the Archaeology and History of the Levant 2 (Winona Lake, IN: Eisenbrauns, 2001).

3. Patrick Nolan and Gerhard Lenski, *Human Societies: An Introduction to Macrosociology*, 10th ed. (Boulder, CO: Paradigm, 2005), copyright page.

that we will explore many of the characteristics of the texts in the chapters that follow. In those chapters, we will examine how these texts convey an account of the past that works as a story, how they portray interests through how that story is shaped, and how they function as historical writing. For now, we focus on the background that is inherent in the texts and the story that is related against that background.

Geographical and Political Context and the Story in Summary: Part 1

When we start looking at the context for the biblical accounts of the past, it is clear that the biblical historical books were aware of and referred to the land and environment in which events took place.[4] As with most adults today, who might read a newspaper or scan a news website to find out what is happening, there was an awareness of the place where they lived and of the larger world that had an impact on their lives and livelihood. One big difference between a connected adult today and one in ancient Israel is the type of connections each had—word of mouth, news in the local market from a traveling tradesperson, and occasional public or royal announcements were the ancient forms of television news and websites!

A word of explanation is needed about the term "Israel." In its most general usage, "Israel" identifies the whole people and community that is the focus of the Old Testament, as in the phrase "people of ancient Israel." However, "Israel" was also the name of the northern state of the two states that developed in the land. In this more specific usage, Israel is often mentioned with Judah, the southern state. We will try to be clear about which meaning is intended when the term is used.

4. For information about the geographical and political context of ancient Israel, see, e.g., J. Maxwell Miller and John H. Hayes, *A History of Ancient Israel and Judah*, 2nd ed. (Philadelphia: Westminster, 2006); Michael D. Coogan, *The Old Testament: A Historical and Literary Introduction to the Hebrew Scriptures* (New York: Oxford University Press, 2011); Nadav Na'aman, *Ancient Israel and Its Neighbours: Interaction and Counteraction*, Collected Essays, vol. 1 (Winona Lake, IN: Eisenbrauns, 2005).

Let's start with the most local context, the land itself. In the book of Deuteronomy, which serves in some ways as an introduction to the Deuteronomistic History (see discussion above in the introduction), we read a description of the land inhabited by the people of ancient Israel: "the hill country of the Amorites as well as . . . the neighboring regions—the Arabah, the hill country, the Shephelah, the Negeb, and the seacoast" (Deut. 1:7). This quote reflecting a setting in the land describes various regions, including geographical zones that generally run north–south, and from east to west they are identified: the "Arabah," or rift valley of the Jordan River and Dead Sea; the central ridge of hills and mountains; the "Shephelah," or foothills between the central hills and seacoast; and the generally low and flat seacoast. Two other regions are mentioned: the more northern hill country "of the Amorites," generally on the east side of the Jordan River, and the Negeb, which was the southernmost dry wilderness area.

Various texts also convey some of the ways the land would be used to sustain the life of the people who lived there. Because ancient Israel was an agricultural area, the main activities of life were farming

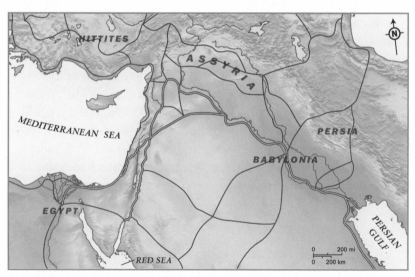

Major Empires in the Ancient Near East (International Mapping)

crops like wheat, barley, grapes, olives, and various other vegetables and fruits, and herding sheep, goats, and cattle. The following verse describes the military, pastoral, and agricultural activities of one of the kings of Judah, which reflects this same agricultural emphasis: "He built towers in the wilderness and hewed out many cisterns, for he had large herds, both in the Shephelah and in the plain, and he had farmers and vinedressers in the hills and in the fertile lands" (2 Chron. 26:10).

This environment of the land could also be described politically, that is, as land that is divided up into territories associated with respective tribes or the states of Israel and Judah. This excerpt from Joshua describing the boundaries of the areas allotted to the tribes reflects a combination of geographical and political awareness about the land:

> [Judah's] south boundary ran from the end of the Dead Sea. . . . And the east boundary is the Dead Sea, to the mouth of the Jordan. And the boundary on the north side runs from the bay of the sea at the mouth of the Jordan; . . . then the boundary goes up by the valley of the son of Hinnom at the southern slope of the Jebusites (that is, Jerusalem); . . . and the boundary circles west of Baalah to Mount Seir, . . . then the boundary comes to an end at the [Mediterranean] sea. (Josh. 15:2, 5, 8, 10–11)

While the texts mostly take for granted that the land was just there as the natural setting of the accounts, the historical books are more deliberate in conveying information about the political entities that inhabited and controlled the land. The presence of the clans and tribes and then later the states of Israel and Judah on the land, along with their various fortunes in either holding or losing the land, occupy much of the stories recounted. Thus the political context of life on the land is woven throughout the account of the past in the historical books.

The historical books ground the story of the land in a foundation tradition that recounts their ancestors—Abraham and Sarah, Isaac and Rebekah, Jacob and Leah and Rachel—coming from the east and interacting with peoples already in the land. The remembered foundation tradition continues with the story of the Israelites' seeking refuge in Egypt during a time of famine and how that sojourn later became a time of slavery in Egypt. The story takes a dramatic turn when the people, under the leadership of Moses and Aaron, make a daring escape from Pharaoh's armies through God's intervention and power. This whole foundation tradition is reflected at the end of the book of Joshua, in a passage where Joshua is portrayed as giving a speech full of traditions and memories:

> And Joshua said to all the people, "Thus says the LORD, the God of Israel: Long ago your ancestors . . . lived beyond the Euphrates and served other gods. Then I took your father Abraham from beyond the River and led him through all the land of Canaan and made his offspring many. . . . Jacob and his children went down to Egypt. Then I sent Moses and Aaron, and I plagued Egypt with what I did in its midst. . . . When I brought your ancestors out of Egypt, you came to the sea; and the Egyptians pursued your ancestors with chariots and horsemen to the Red Sea. When they cried out to the LORD, he . . . made the sea come upon them and cover them." (Josh. 24:2–7)

The foundation tradition continues with the crucial remembrance of the people under Moses's leadership meeting God at a mountain in the wilderness and receiving the teaching and law that would constitute their community under and with God. Including the central Ten Commandments inscribed on stone tablets that Moses received, the covenant was a set of laws that instituted the ways the people had to relate to God and to one another to act out the grace they had received from God in the deliverance from Egypt. The history writing remembers this foundational event:

> The LORD had made a covenant with them and commanded them, "You shall not worship other gods or bow yourselves to them or serve them or sacrifice to them, but you shall worship the LORD, who brought you out of the land of Egypt with great power and with an outstretched arm; you shall bow yourselves to him, and to him you

shall sacrifice. The statutes and the ordinances and the law and the commandment that he wrote for you, you shall always be careful to observe." (2 Kings 17:35–37)

The historical books that we are studying pick up this story line in the books of Joshua and Judges and relate stories of the emergence of the people of Israel in the hill country. Numerous stories and traditions that lay behind these books chronicled the interactions of their clans and tribes with the peoples who lived there, remembering both warfare and local treaties. Here are two examples:

Joshua turned back at that time, and took Hazor, and struck its king down with the sword. Before that time Hazor was the head of all those kingdoms. (Josh. 11:10)

Manasseh did not drive out the inhabitants of Beth-shean and its villages, or Taanach and its villages, . . . or the inhabitants of Megiddo and its villages; but the Canaanites continued to live in that land. When Israel grew strong, they put the Canaanites to forced labor, but did not in fact drive them out. (Judg. 1:27–28)

Then the books of 1 and 2 Samuel relate the rise of the monarchy and how a more organized state slowly developed from the clans and tribes, as political changes both within the area and beyond the local area affected the people and their institutions. The account of the reign of the first king, Saul, relates his rise to power among the tribes of the northern hill country and his battles against the Philistines and other foes.

So all the people went to Gilgal, and there they made Saul king before the LORD in Gilgal. There they sacrificed offerings of well-being before the LORD, and there Saul and all the Israelites rejoiced greatly. (1 Sam. 11:15)

When Saul had taken the kingship over Israel, he fought against all his enemies on every side—against Moab, against the Ammonites, against Edom, . . . and against the Philistines; wherever he turned he routed them. (1 Sam. 14:47)

However, the story recounts how Saul and the northern tribes
he represented did not hold on to power, as a rival, David, pulled
away from Saul and secured the support of the principal southern
tribe, Judah. Though the story is shaped to highlight the theological
aspects of David's rise and eventual kingship (which we will explore
in later chapters), the political outlines of the story portray his power
and ability to unite the northern and southern tribes.

> So David went up [to Hebron]. . . . Then the people of Judah came,
> and there they anointed David king over the house of Judah. (2 Sam.
> 2:2, 4)

> There was a long war between the house of Saul and the house of
> David; David grew stronger and stronger, while the house of Saul
> became weaker and weaker. (2 Sam. 3:1)

> So all the elders of Israel came to the king at Hebron; and King
> David made a covenant with them at Hebron before the LORD, and
> they anointed David king over Israel. . . . At Hebron he reigned over
> Judah for seven years and six months; and at Jerusalem he reigned
> over all Israel and Judah thirty-three years. (2 Sam. 5:3, 5)

As the story line continues in 2 Samuel, David's long rule was
riddled with political intrigue and conflict, but he passed a united
kingdom on to his son Solomon. Solomon is recounted as a wise
and rich king, best known for building the temple in the capital city
of Jerusalem. However, the story relates how his policies of heavy-
handed use of forced labor to build the monumental architecture
of the temple and city cost the kingdom its unity when his son
Rehoboam came to the throne.

> All Israel had come to Shechem to make [Rehoboam] king. . . . Jer-
> oboam [leader of a rebellion] and all the assembly of Israel came
> and said to Rehoboam, "Your father made our yoke heavy. Now
> therefore lighten the hard service of your father and his heavy yoke
> that he placed on us, and we will serve you." . . . The king answered
> the people harshly. . . . "My father made your yoke heavy, but I will

add to your yoke; my father disciplined you with whips, but I will discipline you with scorpions." . . . When all Israel saw that the king would not listen to them, the people answered the king, "What share do we have in David? We have no inheritance in the son of Jesse. To your tents, O Israel! Look now to your own house, O David." . . . So Israel has been in rebellion against the house of David to this day. (1 Kings 12:1, 3–4, 13–14, 16, 19)

The rest of the story of the monarchies in the books of Kings, paralleled extensively in the books of 1 and 2 Chronicles, relates the stories of the separate states of Judah in the south, with its temple and dynasty located in Jerusalem, and Israel in the north, with its capital in Samaria. The history writing in the books of Kings interweaves the stories of the two monarchies, switching back and forth between the reigns of contemporaneous kings over the two hundred years when both states existed.

Geographical and Political Context and the Story in Summary: Part 2

The history written in the story of the monarchies, while focused on Israel and Judah, also situates these states in the international world of the day, because from early on neighboring states along the Mediterranean seacoast interacted with Israel and Judah. In time, states farther away began to have a heavy impact on the people of Israel when the empires of the ancient world took over vast areas of land. The texts of the historical books show awareness of these neighboring states, especially when those states invaded the territory of Judah and Israel.

Besides the Philistines along the seacoast who occupied the tradition's attention during the rise of the monarchy, there were several other small, rival states in the area that interacted with the people of Israel. Ammon, Moab, and Edom were, like Israel and Judah, small agrarian monarchies along the seacoast of the Mediterranean. The northern state of Israel was a stronger and more international-ized state than Judah, in part because its territory included better

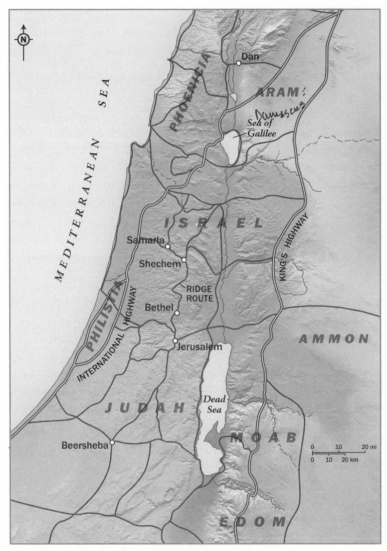

Local Kingdoms around Israel and Judah (International Mapping)

agricultural land and one of the major trade routes. During the
years of the rival monarchies, Israel was able to trade with or dominate its neighbors, including Judah. However, all five of these small
states variously traded, intermarried, or fought among themselves

for political advantage, control, or conquest. For example, Moab, while often recounted as an enemy, is also remembered as the state David sought as a place of refuge for his parents during his political struggles against Saul (1 Sam. 22:3–4). In another example, Solomon married a princess of Ammon among his many political marriages, and it was her son, Rehoboam, who succeeded his father on the throne. Other texts record warfare and rebellion among the states; for example, Edom successfully revolted against the control of Judah at one point (2 Kings 8:20). The tradition also remembers that during part of the time period of the two states, Judah and Israel fought against each other, and Israel dominated Judah in battle (2 Kings 14:11–14).

Two other neighboring states mentioned in the historical books had a particularly large influence on Israel and Judah, as both the texts and social-world studies indicate. The first was the group of seafaring and trading cities of Phoenicia, up the coast from Israel. Both Israel and Judah recounted interactions with Tyre and Sidon, two of Phoenicia's largest cities. The story of Solomon recounts how he asked the king of Tyre for export of the famous cedars of Lebanon and for expertise in skilled metalwork for building the temple, all supported by a trade agreement.

> So Hiram supplied Solomon's every need for timber of cedar and cypress. Solomon in turn gave Hiram twenty thousand cors of wheat as food for his household, and twenty cors of fine oil. Solomon gave this to Hiram year by year. So the LORD gave Solomon wisdom, as he promised him. There was peace between Hiram and Solomon; and the two of them made a treaty. (1 Kings 5:10–12)

The northern state of Israel was particularly tied in with Phoenicia because the two were major trading partners, Israel supplying agricultural products to the coastal cities in exchange for lumber and luxury goods. The strongest alliance came during the ninth century BCE when the dynasty in Israel intermarried with the royal household of Sidon (1 Kings 16:31). The trading pattern of food exports and timber imports with Tyre and Sidon continued into the period

after the Babylonian exile, as the text of Ezra relates in the account
of rebuilding the temple in Jerusalem: "So they gave money to the
masons and the carpenters, and food, drink, and oil to the Sidonians
and the Tyrians to bring cedar trees from Lebanon" (Ezra 3:7).
The relationship of the northern state of Israel with its nearest
north neighbor, Aram (sometimes referred to as Damascus, after its
capital city), is a subject of frequent interest in the history writing
in 1 and 2 Kings. The two states occasionally engaged in trade and
usually in ongoing skirmishes and warfare over territory for over
two centuries. The history writing traces these changing fortunes
within each king's reign.

> Now King Hazael of Aram oppressed Israel all the days of Jeho-
> ahaz. . . . When King Hazael of Aram died, his son Ben-hadad suc-
> ceeded him. Then Jehoash son of Jehoahaz took again from Ben-
> hadad son of Hazael the towns that he had taken from his father
> Jehoahaz in war. Three times Joash defeated him and recovered the
> towns of Israel. (2 Kings 13:22, 24–25)

Around 750 BCE, the context of the biblical world changed dras-
tically with the rise of the Neo-Assyrian Empire, which was the first
of a series of empires that controlled the ancient Near East for the
next four hundred years. With an impact that is widely reflected in
the biblical historical books, these empires changed the international
politics of the whole area, including the domination and conquest
of both Israel and Judah. Under an able ruler, Tiglath-Pileser III
(named King Pul in the biblical texts), the Assyrian state became
an empire over the course of several decades as it conquered territory and required loyalty and tribute from states across to the
Mediterranean.

> King Pul of Assyria came against the land [of Israel]; Menahem gave
> Pul a thousand talents of silver, so that he might help him confirm his
> hold on the royal power. Menahem exacted the money from Israel,
> that is, from all the wealthy, fifty shekels of silver from each one, to
> give to the king of Assyria. So the king of Assyria turned back, and
> did not stay there in the land. (2 Kings 15:19–20)

This respite that Israel won from Assyrian control by becoming a vassal that paid tribute to the empire was only temporary, however. The Assyrians continued to assault and then conquered and destroyed Israel and its capital, Samaria, in 722 BCE. Biblical historiography then recounts the impact of Assyria on Judah, which was subject to an Assyrian assault during the following two decades that destroyed most of its fortified cities. "In the fourteenth year of King Hezekiah, King Sennacherib of Assyria came up against all the fortified cities of Judah and captured them" (2 Kings 18:13). Judah escaped total destruction under King Hezekiah when the Assyrian forces withdrew from a siege against the city of Jerusalem, an account that has received significant attention in the history writing (18:17–19:37). Jerusalem was spared from further assault when Hezekiah became a vassal of the Assyrian Empire, a status that continued under his successor through the next six decades. "The king of Assyria demanded of King Hezekiah of Judah three hundred talents of silver and thirty talents of gold. Hezekiah gave him all the silver that was found in the house of the LORD and in the treasuries of the king's house" (18:14–15).

As the Assyrian Empire weakened in the last decades of the seventh century BCE, other states attempted to pick up the spoils. Egypt, known mostly in the history writing for its oppression of the early Hebrews, had lost its preeminent status for several centuries but now tried to move into the power vacuum among the small states along the Mediterranean. However, the next world power was Babylon, which conquered Assyria, inherited its vast territory, and asserted its own control as the Babylonian Empire. The writing of biblical history shows awareness of these major changes for the story of Judah, chronicling the siege and conquest of Jerusalem.

And in the ninth year of [Zedekiah's] reign, in the tenth month, on the tenth day of the month, King Nebuchadnezzar of Babylon came with all his army against Jerusalem, and laid siege to it; they built siegeworks against it all round. . . . Nebuzaradan, . . . a servant of the king of Babylon, came to Jerusalem. He burned the house of the LORD, the king's house, and all the houses of Jerusalem; every great house he burned down. All the army of the Chaldeans who were with the captain of the guard broke down the walls around Jerusalem. (2 Kings 25:1, 8–10)

The Babylonian Empire, like the Assyrian Empire before it, practiced a policy of deportation and resettlement of conquered peoples to control acquired territories. Second Kings reported this ruinous and final reality for the Davidic monarchy and its capital city, Jerusalem, when its elite population was deported to Babylon in 587 BCE, beginning a time known as the exile. The land of Judah was left as a devastated area, with a remaining population of peasant farmers to carry on basic agricultural work (2 Kings 25:11–12).

The final international context remembered in the historical books of the Old Testament is a time period of recovery from the disaster of the exile. After fifty years, the Babylonian Empire fell to the new power in the east, the Persian Empire. The Persian Empire provides the context for the history writing recorded in the books of Ezra and Nehemiah, which focus on the community that returned from exile to a restored Judah. The account recalls the Persians as well disposed toward the Judean exiles and as sponsoring their return to Judah by the decree of a Persian emperor.

Thus says King Cyrus of Persia: The LORD, the God of heaven, has given me all the kingdoms of the earth, and he has charged me to build him a house at Jerusalem in Judah. Any of those among you who are of his people—may their God be with them!—are now permitted to go up to Jerusalem in Judah, and rebuild the house of the LORD. (Ezra 1:2–3)

Persia stayed in power as an empire for about two hundred years, variously trying to hold Egypt and to conquer Greece. This time period reflects the rest of the context recorded in the historical writings that are our focus. The accounts in Ezra and Nehemiah show awareness of Persia and report how the empire continued its favorable interest in Judah, supporting the leadership of the restored community in Jerusalem through resources for rebuilding the temple and appointment of political leadership. For example, the book of Ezra records a decree by King Darius. "Let the governor of the Jews and the elders of the Jews rebuild this house of God on its site. Moreover I make a decree . . . : the cost is to be paid to these people, in full and without delay, from the royal revenue, the tribute of the province Beyond the River" (Ezra 6:7–8). Along with Ezra's appointment by Persia as recorded in Ezra 7, the book of Nehemiah records that Nehemiah, a Jewish royal servant of the Persian king Artaxerxes, was appointed by Persia to rebuild the walls of Jerusalem and to govern the province as a Persian appointee. "Then I said to the king, 'If it pleases the king, and if your servant has found favor with you, I ask that you send me to Judah, to the city of my ancestors' graves, so that I may rebuild it.' . . . So it pleased the king to send me" (Neh. 2:5–6).

For convenience, the following chart presents a summary of this overview. The events and main characters of biblical history writing are represented against a timeline that indicates the approximate dates that correspond to the context of the ancient world. Further, the international players that were referenced in the accounts of the historical writing are represented at their approximate time in the third column.

Religious Context of the History Writing

Moving from the political context of biblical history writing to its religious context is not a big step, because the political and religious realms were highly intertwined in ancient times. You may be familiar with the idea of "separation of church and state," but that idea had no presence in the ancient world. In fact, quite the opposite was true. All ancient societies understood that they lived as a part of a cosmos that was controlled by a god or gods. Each state had its own pantheon of gods and goddesses and understood that the state, the dynasty, and the temple of that state were intimately connected with the cosmos in which the state existed. The king and dynasty representing the state looked to the gods for the legitimization of

Context and Story in Biblical History Writing

Dates	Biblical Events/People	International Scene
		Egypt dominant over coastal areas (to about 1200 BCE)
	Ancestors	
	(Abraham and Sarah)	
	Refuge in Egypt	
	(Joseph)	
1225 BCE	Exodus from Egypt	
	(Moses and Aaron)	
	Israel emerges in land	Other small states emerge
	(Joshua, the judges) (Samuel, Saul)	Edom, Moab, Ammon, Philistines, Tyre/Sidon develop maritime trade
1000 BCE	United Monarchy	
	(David, Solomon)	
	Temple built	
925 BCE	Division of kingdoms:	
	north/Israel, south/Judah	
	(Rehoboam, Jeroboam)	Aramean pressure (845–785)
	Trade/alliances created	
	(Ahab, Jezebel, Elijah)	
		Assyrian Empire (745–627)
722 BCE	Fall of Samaria/Israel	
	Judah alone, Assyrian vassal	
	(Hezekiah, Isaiah)	
		Babylonian Empire (605–539)
587 BCE	Fall of Jerusalem/Judah	
	Destruction of temple/exile	
	Peasants left on land	
538 BCE	End of exile, Cyrus's edict	Persian Empire (539–333)
	Return of Jews to Judah	
	Rebuilding temple	
	Persian domination	
	(Ezra)	
450 BCE	(Nehemiah)	

their power. The visible confirmation of the gods' presence and authorization for the state was the temple in the capital city, which was built by the king to give physical presence and honor to the gods that upheld the state.[5] Ancient Israel, of course, witnessed that only God was the creator and Lord of the universe and framed its historical writing in that understanding, but its understanding fit against this background of religion in its world and time.

As we did in the previous section, we will explore the religious context of biblical historical writings from within the texts themselves. By doing this we can see how the historical writings imaged their own religious reality. We can start with the fundamental perception that kingship, dynasty, and temple were linked with God's presence and power. In a passage that portrays this central religious reality of the Davidic dynasty, 2 Samuel 7 reports the word King David heard from God about his decision to build a temple in Jerusalem. The story tells how after David had built his own house (the palace) and wanted to build the house of God (the temple), the prophet Nathan spoke God's message.

> Go and tell my servant David: Thus says the LORD: Are you the one to build me a house to live in? . . . The LORD declares to you that the LORD will make you a house. When your days are fulfilled and you lie down with your ancestors, I will raise up your offspring after you, who shall come forth from your body, and I will establish his kingdom. He shall build a house for my name, and I will establish the throne of his kingdom forever. (2 Sam. 7:5, 11–13)

5. For further understanding about the religion of ancient Israel, see the classic study by Henri Frankfort, *Kingship and the Gods: A Study of Ancient Near Eastern Religion as the Integration of Society and Nature* (Chicago: University of Chicago Press, 1948), as well as Patrick D. Miller, *The Religion of Ancient Israel* (Louisville: Westminster John Knox, 2000); Moshe Weinfeld, "Zion and Jerusalem as Religious and Political Capital: Ideology and Utopia," in *The Poet and the Historian: Essays in Literary and Historical Biblical Criticism*, ed. Richard Elliott Friedman (Chico, CA: Scholars Press, 1983), 75–115; Victor Avigdor Hurowitz, *I Have Built You an Exalted House: Temple Building in the Bible in the Light of Mesopotamian and North-West Semitic Writings*, Journal for the Study of the Old Testament Supplement Series 115 (Sheffield: JSOT Press, 1992); and Mark S. Smith, *The Early History of God: Yahweh and the Other Deities in Ancient Israel* (San Francisco: Harper & Row, 1990).

This passage imaginatively uses a triple pun on the Hebrew word for "house," which also works in English: the house of the king (his palace), the house of the king's family line (his dynasty), and the house of God (the temple). The context of both the pun and the religious politics behind the passage is exactly the one we noted for the ancient world: the close and legitimizing relationship among the cosmic God, the king and his dynasty, and the temple, which is the house the king builds for the god of the state.

The books of Kings and Chronicles reflect this same political and religious connection throughout, but particularly in the report on the founding of the northern state of Israel under Jeroboam. Once he has achieved power, Jeroboam is portrayed as understanding that he must establish the northern state's own religious center to legitimize and centralize his rule. First Kings 12 reports his thinking and his subsequent actions.

> "If this people continues to go up to offer sacrifices in the house of the LORD at Jerusalem, the heart of this people will turn again to their master, King Rehoboam of Judah; they will kill me and return to King Rehoboam of Judah." So the king took counsel, and made two calves of gold. . . . He set one in Bethel, and the other he put in Dan. . . . He went up to the altar that he had made in Bethel . . . and he went up to the altar to offer incense. (1 Kings 12:27–29, 33)

These sanctuaries established by Jeroboam in the northern kingdom were considered illegitimate and a source of sinful religious practice, and they are regularly condemned in the history writing. The temple in Jerusalem became the center of religious focus for Judah in the centuries after its founding by Solomon. And in the centuries after the exile, when the temple was rebuilt, it provided a center for the whole community of restored Judah, especially because the political dynasty could not be reestablished under Persian occupation. The temple had been built on a high point in the geography of Jerusalem, and the hill it crowned was known as Zion, a name that occurs regularly in the poetry and prophecy of the Old Testament. The temple symbolized the very presence of God's glory and name in the midst of the people. The spiritual and sacred quality of the temple is conveyed in the account about bringing the ark into the newly built temple.

> Then the priests brought the ark of the covenant of the LORD to its place, in the inner sanctuary of the house, in the most holy place. . . . There was nothing in the ark except the two tablets of stone that Moses had placed there at Horeb, where the LORD made a covenant with the Israelites, when they came out of the land of Egypt. And when the priests came out of the holy place, a cloud filled the house of the LORD, so that the priests could not stand to minister because of the cloud; for the glory of the LORD filled the house of the LORD. (1 Kings 8:6, 9–11)

In addition to the intersections of divine and human realities in the political and religious realms, another basic religious concept of the context of ancient Israel was an understanding of holiness. Holiness, a central concept of reality for ancient Israel, expressed both the ultimate revered and sacrosanct quality of God and the idea that God had ordered the cosmos into two states of being, that which was specially set apart to be holy, or sacred, and the rest of reality, which was common or ordinary. Further, anything that was contrary to holiness was considered unclean or impure. In the same way that the cosmos was separated into distinct spheres of holiness and ordinariness, the created human realm was also understood as differentiated into different states, distinguishing purity from impurity, life from death, clean from unclean, order from chaos, and wholeness from partiality or mixture. While the following quote is from Leviticus, outside the historical books, it expresses the basic ideal of holiness in the people's lives:

> I am the LORD your God; I have separated you from the peoples. You shall therefore make a distinction between the clean animal and the unclean, and between the unclean bird and the clean; you shall not bring abomination on yourselves by animal or by bird or by anything with which the ground teems, which I have set apart for you to hold unclean. You shall be holy to me; for I the LORD

am holy, and I have separated you from the other peoples to be
mine. (Lev. 20:24–26)

The practices of Israelite religion reflected holiness. For example,
in the quote given above about bringing the ark into the temple,
the holiness of God is described as "glory" that was so powerful
that the priests could not be too close to it. The daily rituals of
life respected and embodied the distinctions of holiness, so that
even ordinary actions, such as choosing foods, practicing healing
and medicine, and ordering family relationships, were supposed to
reflect the distinctions of holiness and avoid impurity. The writing
in the historical books reflects this understanding both in indirect
ways and sometimes with a very direct reference. For example, in
this account of crossing the Jordan River into the land, which is
visualized as a sacred and ritual action, the leaders warn the people
about the holiness of the ark of the covenant and how they must be
pure in the presence of God:

> "When you see the ark of the covenant of the LORD your God being
> carried by the levitical priests, then you shall set out from your
> place. . . . Yet there shall be a space between you and it, a distance
> of about two thousand cubits; do not come any nearer to it." Then
> Joshua said to the people, "Sanctify yourselves; for tomorrow the
> LORD will do wonders among you." (Josh. 3:3–5)

In addition to showing the connection between the divine realm
and the political realm, and conveying the importance of holiness,
religion in the ancient world also played an important role as the
set of practices by which human worshipers expressed their reverence toward and dependence on the divine. Religious life for ancient
Israel had both a centralized and a local focus. The texts regularly
express how the temple was the central focal point of worship for
the people of the nation. Here the priests led worshipers in sacrifices and offerings, rituals that marked agricultural festivals and expressed reverence, thanksgiving, and repentance. The people partici-
pated through offering prayers, bringing donations for appropriate

sacrifices, and contributing to support the temple and its personnel. These rituals embodied and symbolized the connections between the people and God and maintained the distinctions of holiness so that the people would be religiously acceptable to God. Looking back to Aaron, the first priest named in the foundation tradition, the texts of Samuel and Kings recall that under David two priests representing their priestly families had shared religious leadership, Zadok and Ahimelech son of Abiathar (2 Sam. 8:17). The priests of ancient Israel receive special attention in the books of Chronicles and Ezra, which are careful to convey the reestablishment of proper worship in the rebuilt temple (Ezra 6:18). First Chronicles expresses a concern to extend legitimization to the Levites as an order of the priesthood during David's reign. As the text recalls, the Levites were instituted by David's order.

> And [the Levites] shall stand every morning, thanking and praising the LORD, and likewise at evening, and whenever burnt offerings are offered to the LORD on sabbaths, new moons, and appointed festivals, according to the number required of them, regularly before the LORD. Thus they shall keep charge of the tent of meeting and the sanctuary, and shall attend the descendants of Aaron, their kindred, for the service of the house of the LORD. (1 Chron. 23:30–32)

In addition to worshiping at the temple centrally located in Jerusalem, people in the towns and villages of Israel and Judah also worshiped at local sanctuaries throughout much of the period of the preexilic monarchy. In these local cult sites, a priestly family would maintain the small worship site and conduct sacrifices, burn incense, and hear prayers. Often on a hilltop near a village or town, or near the gates of a fortified city, these local sanctuaries were linked to the rhythm of life in the countryside. A number of such local holy places are mentioned in the historical writings. For example, this passage tells simply about the regular worship at such a site: "Now this man [from the hill country of Ephraim] used to go up year by year from his town to worship and to sacrifice to the LORD of hosts at Shiloh, where the two sons of Eli, Hophni and Phinehas, were priests of the LORD" (1 Sam. 1:3).

In historical writings that emerged later in the preexilic time period and in the postexilic period, such local sanctuaries are recognized as part of the life of the people but are condemned as drawing the

Social Contexts in History Writing

As in the examples below, modern histories often include information about the social, economic, and environmental contexts to help set the scene for historical events.

This text describes Founding Father John Adams's journey from Boston to Philadelphia in January 1776:

> At New York, horses and riders would be ferried over the Hudson River to New Jersey. . . . Three more ferry crossings, at Hackensack, Newark, and New Brunswick, would put them on a straightaway ride to the little college town of Princeton. . . . All told, they would pass through more than fifty towns in five provinces. . . . With ice clogging the rivers, there was no estimating how long the delays might be at ferry crossings.[a]

Here is a description of the social and economic changes that preceded the Civil War, particularly the growth of railroads:

> These marvels [steamboats, railroads, telegraph] profoundly altered American life. . . . Towns bypassed by [railroad] tracks shriveled; those located on the iron boomed. . . . Racing at breakneck speeds of thirty miles per hour, the iron horse cut travel time between New York and Chicago from three weeks to two days.[b]

The dugout house described in this passage was inhabited by one of the Dustbowl survivors of the High Plains during the Great Depression:

> A dugout is just that—a hole dug into the hide of the prairie. The floor was dirt. Above ground, the walls were plank boards with no insulation on the inside and black tarpaper on the outside. Every spring, Ike's mother poured boiling water over the walls to kill fresh-hatched bugs. . . . The toilet was outside, a hole in the ground.[c]

a. David McCullough, *John Adams* (New York: Simon and Schuster, 2001), 23.
b. James McPherson, *Battle Cry of Freedom: The Civil War Era*, Oxford History of the United States 6 (New York: Oxford University Press, 1988), 12.
c. Timothy Egan, *The Worst Hard Time: The Untold Story of Those Who Survived the Great American Dustbowl* (New York: Houghton Mifflin, 2006), 4.

people away from a required focus on the temple in Jerusalem. The local sanctuaries are also often seen as keeping alive worship of the gods of the previous inhabitants of the land, the Canaanite god Baal and goddess Asherah. Baal worship in particular is targeted in the historical writings as an aberration from the exclusive worship of the Lord. Using the term "high places," which refers to the sites usually situated on a hill, the writing expresses its theological interests in evaluating kings by whether they did or did not destroy the local sanctuaries and the worship of Baal. (We will explore this further when we consider the "interests" of the text in chap. 3.) Here is one such royal evaluation: "He did what was right in the sight of the LORD, yet not like his ancestor David; in all things he did as his father Joash had done. But the high places were not removed; the people still sacrificed and made offerings on the high places" (2 Kings 14:3–4).

The religious sphere of ancient Israel as it is conveyed in the historical writings includes one other important aspect of life: the role of the prophets. The writing expresses the role of the prophets to be that of bringing a message from the divine realm to the leaders of the political and religious life of Israel and Judah. This role also fits well in the context of the ancient world, where other societies also recognized the position of visionaries or seers who brought a word from the gods to kings and priests. In the history writing, prophets often communicate their critique or support of actions and attitudes, and through this the texts show how God intervened and communicated with the kings and other leaders of the state. The following passages show two examples of prophetic communication in the historical texts:

When [King] Ahab saw [the prophet] Elijah, Ahab said to him, "Is it you, you troubler of Israel?" He answered, "I have not troubled Israel; but you have, and your father's house, because you have forsaken the commandments of the LORD and followed the Baals." (1 Kings 18:17–18)

Now the prophets, Haggai and Zechariah son of Iddo, prophesied to the Jews who were in Judah and Jerusalem, in the name of the God of Israel who was over them. Then [the leaders] set out to rebuild the house of God in Jerusalem; and with them were the prophets of God, helping them. (Ezra 5:1–2)

Social Context of Biblical History Writing

In some ways, the social context of biblical history writing is an invisible background, because the texts usually assume that their audience understands how the families, social roles, groups, and institutions were structured in ancient Israel. Today, we often assume a similar familiarity. When we are composing a text message or talking to a friend, we rarely stop to explain the social institutions like families, governments, schools, and businesses that inhabit our "world." We just assume that our correspondent knows the society in which we live. It is generally only when we are talking with someone from outside our context that we have to stop to explain. Imagine that you are the guide for a foreign exchange student at your school; you would have to do a lot of explaining about many things, such as why almost everyone at your college attends the football or hockey games on the weekend. However, there are traces of and references to the social context in the historical writing, and we will explore the social context by discovering the background that makes sense of those traces and references.[6]

We can start with the most basic social unit in the world of ancient Israel: the family. Notice that we are immediately in a different context from one you might imagine, where you assume that the most basic social unit is the individual. From what we know of ancient Israel, when people reported who they were, they did not first report their individual identity the way a person today might. Rather, individuals thought of themselves first and foremost as members of an extended family. Look at how this person was introduced: "There

6. See Fritz, *The City in Ancient Israel*; McNutt, *Reconstructing the Society of Ancient Israel*; King and Stager, *Life in Biblical Israel*; Carter and Meyers, eds., *Community, Identity, and Ideology*; Chalcraft, ed., *Social-Scientific Old Testament Criticism*; Schloen, *The House of the Father as Fact and Symbol*.

was a certain man of Ramathaim, a Zuphite from the hill country of Ephraim, whose name was Elkanah son of Jeroham son of Elihu son of Tohu son of Zuph, an Ephraimite" (1 Sam. 1:1). This man is identified by his family of origin, tracing his lineage back several generations and placing that family on its ancestral land in the highland hill country. The primary context for the people's livelihood in agriculture, socialization, education, crafts and manufacturing of goods, and health was the family household. Households consisted of the elder generation, usually the patriarchal head of the household and his wife or wives,[7] their unmarried children, their married sons and their sons' wives, and any grandchildren. Daughters married out into their husbands' households. This family unit usually lived together in a compound of connected or adjacent houses, and that household was the primary economic production unit of the society.

Every household was nested inside a larger structure of the clan, a group of households related by blood or marriage, living in geographical proximity and providing an association for the families. Beyond that, larger familial and generational connections linked the clans into tribes, and finally the tribes were part of the state as a whole.[8] Look at the way this passage represents how the Israelites made a decision by selecting a particular clan, then family, then individual from within all the tribes: "In the morning therefore you shall come forward tribe by tribe. The tribe that the LORD takes shall come near by clans, the clan that the LORD takes shall come near by households, and the household that the LORD takes shall come near one by one" (Josh. 7:14). The patriarchal heads of families were accorded honor and status and were looked to for tasks of adjudicating disputes among families, representing the family in the decisions of the village or town, and carrying the family's interests into decisions by the clans.

7. Polygamy was a socially and religiously acceptable cultural pattern throughout Old Testament texts. See the law on the protection of the firstborn son of a second, unloved wife (Deut. 21:15–17), the stories of Rachel and Leah (Gen. 30) and Hannah and Peninnah (1 Sam. 1), as well as the frequent references to multiple royal wives, notably David's (2 Sam. 3:2–5).

8. King and Stager, *Life in Biblical Israel*, 4.

The family household functioned as the basic economic produc-
tive unit of the society. Much of the agricultural and household craft
production was accomplished by both men and women, who divided
work among the married partners, brothers and sisters, and cousins
of the extended household.[9] While women were under the protection and control of the males of the family—their fathers, brothers,
or husbands—they also had significant economic status and roles
in the household livelihood. In 1 Samuel, for example, Abigail, the
wife of a powerful sheepherder in southern Judah, is described as
"clever and beautiful" (1 Sam. 25:3). She is portrayed as commanding
knowledge of the economic resources of the household and is obeyed
by the hired men of the household, and she acts independently of
her husband in coming to David's aid with supplies.

> Then Abigail hurried and took two hundred loaves, two skins of wine,
> five sheep ready dressed, five measures of parched grain, one hundred
> clusters of raisins, and two hundred cakes of figs. She loaded them on
> donkeys and said to her young men, "Go on ahead of me; I am coming
> after you." But she did not tell her husband Nabal. (1 Sam. 25:18–19)

Closely tied into the life of each extended family was the ancestral
land on which they lived. In fact, the livelihood of the whole household was dependent on the land and its crops in the largely agrarian
society of ancient Israel. One text in 2 Kings reports the crops of
the land: "a land of grain and wine, a land of bread and vineyards,
a land of olive oil and honey" (18:32). A variety of crops provided
a varied diet and allowed the household a measure of protection
against agricultural risks of drought and blight, which endangered
food supplies and the household's ability to pay its taxes and debts.
Crop damage from "blight, mildew, locust, or caterpillar" (1 Kings
8:37) brought risks to harvests. Drought was a constant threat that
could result in starvation for the poor who had no other protection ·
when their crops failed. During a drought, the prophet Elijah was
sent to a poor widow, who describes her plight: "As the LORD your

9. See especially Carol Meyers, *Discovering Eve: Ancient Israelite Women in Context* (New York: Oxford University Press, 1988).

God lives, I have nothing baked, only a handful of meal in a jar, and a little oil in a jug; I am now gathering a couple of sticks, so that I may go home and prepare it for myself and my son, that we may eat it, and die" (1 Kings 17:12).

In several other passages, the importance of land for the peasant farmers of ancient Israel is traced. In another prophetic story, a woman who sought refuge in another land during a time of famine is shown returning and having to appeal to the king to get her house and land restored to her (2 Kings 8:1–6). Another story depicts the response of an Israelite landholder when King Ahab asked to acquire his land, which was near the palace. The man is portrayed as being unable to even conceive of giving away his ancestral inheritance. "But Naboth said to Ahab, 'The LORD forbid that I should give you my ancestral inheritance'" (1 Kings 21:3).

The land of ancient Israel was also organized socially to fit the needs of the people. Household lands were distributed around the land of a local village, which might contain several extended families and their landholdings in fields, vineyards, orchards, and pastureland. The village might have been protected by a low stone wall to keep out predators and keep in livestock. The next level of organization would have been towns, where other households also lived, and where there would have been a local market for the area and perhaps the protection of a larger defensive wall. The largest social habitations were cities. Though small in population by our standards, with a population in the thousands even for a substantial city, the cities were protected by major defensive walls and included significant marketplaces and cisterns for water storage, as well as governmental, commercial, and military buildings. The historical texts report this arrangement of families, villages, towns, and cities in descriptions from both before and after the exile.

> This is the inheritance of the tribe of Issachar, according to its families—the towns with their villages. (Josh. 19:23)

> This is the account of the forced labor that King Solomon conscripted to build the house of the LORD and his own house, the

Millo and the wall of Jerusalem, Hazor, Megiddo, Gezer . . . as well as all of Solomon's storage cities, the cities for his chariots, the cities for his cavalry, and whatever Solomon desired to build, in Jerusalem, in Lebanon, and in all the land of his dominion. (1 Kings 9:15, 19)

And the rest of Israel, and of the priests and the Levites, were in all the towns of Judah, all of them in their inheritance. . . . And as for the villages, with their fields, some of the people of Judah lived in Kiriath-arba and its villages, and in Dibon and its villages, and in Jekabzeel and its villages. (Neh. 11:20, 25)

A final social reality that underlies the historical writing of the Old Testament is the stratification of society into rich and poor classes. As in a typical agrarian society, there was a large gap between the very few who were the richest members of the social structure (the king and the governing elite) and the numerous poorest members (the peasant farmers). The structures of the extended families supported the well-being of peasant farmers, but some experienced starvation in years of bad harvests. Very few people, perhaps some skilled artisans and merchants, would have been in what we could call a "middle class." In part, you can see this reality in the description of the villages, towns, and cities: people with wealth and status often lived in the cities. Much of the economy was heavily influenced by the actions and control of the elites from the royal household and its representatives through taxation, acquisition of land, and the imposition of duties on trade. The description of the final days of Judah indirectly witnesses to this social structure as it reflected the makeup of the elite classes that were deported in contrast to the peasants who were left on the land.

[The king of Babylon] carried away all Jerusalem, all the officials, all the warriors, ten thousand captives, all the artisans and the smiths; no one remained, except the poorest people of the land. He carried away Jehoiachin to Babylon; the king's mother, the king's wives, his officials, and the elite of the land, he took into captivity from Jerusalem to Babylon. (2 Kings 24:14–15)

The social and economic relationships between the rich and the poor often worked to the advantage of the wealthy and powerful. The most debilitating reality for the poor was the all-too-frequent need to borrow in order to maintain their agricultural activities. Such debt could become a burden that could not be paid back if a harvest failed due to drought or blight, and interest rates increased the debt burden. Peasants who could not repay a loan were in danger of falling into debt slavery or losing their land. Such realities are reflected in the historical writings. One story records the vulnerability of a family whom the prophet Elisha later helped. "Now the wife of a member of the company of prophets cried to Elisha, 'Your servant my husband is dead; and you know that your servant feared the LORD, but a creditor has come to take my two children as slaves'" (2 Kings 4:1).

In the postexilic period, such realities remained, according to a passage in Nehemiah in which he is shown dealing with a situation of famine that caused poverty and indebtedness.

> There were also those who said, "We are having to pledge our fields, our vineyards, and our houses in order to get grain during the famine." And there were those who said, "We are having to borrow money on our fields and vineyards to pay the king's tax." . . . [Nehemiah said to the nobles,] "Restore to them, this very day, their fields, their vineyards, their olive orchards, and their houses, and the interest on money, grain, wine, and oil that you have been exacting from them." (Neh. 5:3–4, 11)

Note that the final verse cited also gives a good description of a family household's agricultural resources in the society of ancient Israel.

Conclusion

The numerous quotes from the historical writing of the Old Testament show how the political, religious, and social contexts of the writing were both the background for the story and included in the texts. These realities were the ordinary environment and backdrop of the writing, almost "invisible," and yet they powerfully shaped the life of the people and the way that life has been portrayed in the texts. These political, religious, and social contexts will keep cropping up throughout the rest of our examination of the historical writing. Now that you are attuned to what these contexts are, you will be able to see them as they work in the background of the texts we examine. As we turn in the next chapter to see how historical writing works as narrative artistry, these contexts will be woven through the stories we consider.

Suggested Reading

Coogan, Michael D. "The Promised Land: Geography, History and Importance." Pages 11–27 in *A Historical and Literary Introduction to the Hebrew Scriptures*. 2nd ed. New York: Oxford University Press, 2011.

Frankfort, Henri. *Kingship and the Gods: A Study of Ancient Near Eastern Religion as the Integration of Society and Nature*. Chicago: University of Chicago Press, 1978.

King, Philip J., and Lawrence E. Stager. *Life in Biblical Israel*. Library of Ancient Israel. Louisville: Westminster John Knox, 2001.

McNutt, Paula. *Reconstructing the Society of Ancient Israel*. Library of Ancient Israel. Louisville: Westminster John Knox, 1999.

Miller, J. Maxwell, and John H. Hayes. *A History of Ancient Israel and Judah*. 2nd ed. Philadelphia: Westminster, 2006.

Miller, Patrick D. *The Religion of Ancient Israel*. Louisville: Westminster John Knox, 2000.

Discussion Questions

1. Try an experiment: relate one of the family stories you have heard about your ancestors to one of your friends. Notice what kinds of things you have to explain because they are not self-evident to your friend in their context today. Would you have to do a little research to explain these things well?

2. Have you or anyone in your classes or social group ever lived in a very rural area—for example, in a small town in an agricultural area or in a village in another part of the world, particularly a developing country? Ask that person to describe what life is like in a small village or rural area. How does their story contrast with the upbringing of someone from a city or suburban area?

3. What are the biggest differences between your life and context and the life and context of a family in ancient Israel? What aspects of that ancient life will you most keep in mind as you read Old Testament texts?

2

Listening to the Story in the Text

If you were to read almost any text from the biblical historical books without knowing that it came from the Bible, you would probably assume that it is a story, because it sounds like a story you might read in other types of literature. The story has a beginning and an end that satisfies you as a reader in hearing a complete tale. There is a plot, so interesting problems or conflicts are set out for a main character whose actions are advanced or thwarted by other characters, and events are finally brought to a crisis and conclusion. There are characters; some are major ones who do and say a lot and are well described by words or actions, while others are minor ones who just have "walk-on" roles. Different points of view are presented; mostly you read what the narrator or storyteller has to say from his or her perspective, but sometimes you hear about events or people from the perspective of one of the characters. Time passes slowly or quickly while events pass by in great detail or in summary format. In short, you will realize that you have read a story not unlike other stories you have read.

This insight into the type of literature that the biblical historical books present to the reader is an important part of taking the text seriously. We can assume that the creators of the biblical historical books went to some lengths to make their writing "work" as story, since the various texts seem carefully crafted. The format seems to be a deliberate choice that conveys what the writers wanted to say to their audiences—those who were readers and listeners for these stories. So it is our job as readers to take the story format of the texts seriously and to listen carefully to these ancient stories.

Stories sometimes are fictional—made up by a writer from his or her imagination. However, stories also are the format we use to relate what we call nonfiction. You probably are familiar with the power of stories to recall the past, to evoke insight and emotions, to keep memories alive, and to relate events. Perhaps you have listened to stories from your family about your ancestors that tell about important events in your family's past. Such a story from a grandparent might even begin, "I remember when I was little . . . ," and might go on to relate an event that was important for that person and for your family. Such stories speak truth about who you are, who your family is, and how you came to be who you are and to think about your family. Or if you ask friends what they did on their vacation, they will likely tell you stories about their activities. You have read a lot of stories, from the novels and short stories you read for fun to those assigned in literature classes. You have read stories in history books, on blogs and websites, and in newspapers. You also know stories that are told through movies and television shows where sometimes the story runs across a series of shows or movies, so that a long story arc is told. Stories are the way we interact with the world when we want to tell about something that has happened.

These commonalities about stories and their impact on human life mean that reading biblical stories can seem easy. However, the way ancient stories were told is not exactly the same as the ways modern stories, fictional or nonfictional, are told. There are different conventions, formats, and expectations for a modern story that do not apply for ancient stories. Perhaps the most important difference that will affect how you read these stories is that biblical narrative tends to be spare—biblical writers use very few words to tell their tales, being very economical in relating exactly what is needed and no more. The difference between a modern novel full of description and a biblical story with few details is like the difference between long essays on a blog and a text message. In reading a text message you know that every word, even every character, is important. So too with biblical narrative—any information given is likely to be important in some way. Listening carefully to the text of the biblical historical books, learning to read the stories well, includes learning how biblical stories have been put together. How did ancient storytellers work their art, and what did ancient audiences expect from a story?[1]

Plot Development: General Characteristics

Plot is the architecture of a story—the structure on which other story elements are built. Plot development involves events that unfold as the story is told, what "happens" in the story. Many contemporary tales are plot heavy—that is, they are principally built around an exciting or intriguing series of events that hold a reader's interest. The latest popular science fiction narratives, vampire stories, and crime dramas, whether in books, movies, or television, tend to emphasize plot and action. In contrast, you may know of some stories, novels, or movies that are centered on character development; not much happens in these tales, but rather the audience learns a lot about the interior and exterior lives of the characters. However, much of modern media works to relate plot. If you watch a television series, each episode has a plot within it, which captures your attention for that hour. However, the series as a whole also makes sense, so the plot has to extend over the whole season or several seasons. Other elements of stories, like character or timing, will be worked into

1. This review of biblical narrative art is based on studies such as Robert Alter, *The Art of Biblical Narrative* (New York: Basic Books, 1981); Shimon Bar-Efrat, *Narrative Art in the Bible* (Sheffield: Almond, 1989); David M. Gunn, "Narrative Criticism," in *To Each Its Own Meaning*, ed. Steven R. Haynes and Steven L. McKenzie, rev. ed. (Louisville: Westminster John Knox, 1999), 201–29; and Yairah Amit, *Reading Biblical Narratives* (Minneapolis: Fortress, 2001).

the plot and will add to the effect of the whole, but the focus will be on incidents that make up the plot.

Plot Development: Beginnings and Endings

To see how plot development works in typical stories from the biblical historical books, we will first examine a story from Judges 4. (It would be helpful to read the whole story for yourself, as we will only excerpt it here.) This story can be used to illustrate how biblical stories characteristically start and end, and how they build scenes. As you read and analyze biblical stories, it might be helpful to imagine that you are a movie director who is turning the narrative into a movie and thus has to plan the scenes to be shot by the cameras. Thinking about how each scene works, where it is set, what actors are in the scene, and what the transitions are between scenes will help you visualize how stories work.

Questions for Careful Readers

Where are the beginning and end of the narrative?

How are these marked?

Is the narrative part of a larger story or ongoing story line?

Biblical narrative uses a variety of ways to start a story, often with a phrase like "At that time . . ." or "After these things . . ." or "Now the people had gathered at the mountain . . ." or "When the king heard. . . ." These and other phrases are markers to signal that a new tale or a new chapter of an ongoing tale is beginning. In almost all cases a story begins when there is a change in time, setting, or characters from what came before. In some cases where a series of stories is linked, similar to the episodes of a television series, a particular phrase will be repeated at the beginning of each story. Biblical narrative is often quite clear about the endings of stories as well, just as the phrase "and they all lived happily ever after" lets you know that a fairy tale is done. Biblical stories typically conclude by giving a summary that directly informs the reader that the conflict or problem of the story's plot has been resolved. Other types of endings include notations that some element of the story, such as a name, character, or place, continues to be famous in later years in Israel.

Look now at the story in Judges 4, which begins,

> The Israelites again did what was evil in the sight of the LORD. . . .
> So the LORD sold them into the hand of King Jabin of Canaan,
> who reigned in Hazor; the commander of his army was Sisera. . . .
> Then the Israelites cried out to the LORD for help; for he had nine
> hundred chariots of iron, and had oppressed the Israelites cruelly
> twenty years. (Judg. 4:1–3)

And the story ends, "So on that day God subdued King Jabin of
Canaan before the Israelites. Then the hand of the Israelites bore
harder and harder on King Jabin of Canaan, until they destroyed
King Jabin of Canaan" (4:23–24). You can see in these excerpts a
typical beginning and ending of a story in biblical narrative. In this
case, the "again" in the opening verse alerts you that a similar story
or stories have preceded this one. In fact, this is one of a series of
stories set in the time when Israel was emerging in the land of Canaan and confronting challenges and enemies. (In later chapters, we
will examine the use of such a repeated pattern as a way to shape
the interests of the story and how the events are remembered as history.) The phrase, however, also lets the audience know that a new
tale in the series is beginning. This narrative opening introduces the
character of King Jabin of Hazor, one of the major cities in Canaan,
and describes the military threat he poses to the Israelites because
he has chariots of iron, a piece of military technology at the time
that gave a distinct advantage if the other side did not have chariots.
Also, even without knowing the middle sections of the story, you
can see from these excerpts how the ending wraps up and completes
the tale, typical of biblical narrative. We are told that the immediate
military threat has been subdued, and we are given a brief forward
look to the time when this king will pose no further menace at all.

Plot Development: Scenic Structure

In considering scene structure, we again can see the characteristics
of biblical narrative.

**Questions
for Careful Readers**

What events/scenes take place?

Who is in each scene?

What are the transitions between scenes?

Scenes in biblical narratives generally change when one or more of several
things happens: a time change occurs, a
different pacing of time is started, a new
character or characters come "on stage,"
or the setting changes to a new place. If
you are imagining a movie, it is at these
junctures that you as a director would
need to start a new section of the movie and perhaps think about
new scenery, new characters, or a way to portray a later time in the
story (or earlier, in the case of a flashback). Within any one scene in
biblical narrative, the characters on stage tend to be limited—usually only two major characters are engaged in action and dialogue,
although there may be numerous minor characters who have only
a very limited speaking role, if any. Scenes in biblical narrative can
range from one or two verses up to ten or twenty verses. Usually
new chapter numbers and sometimes new paragraphs in an English
translation correspond to scene changes.

If we now look for how the scenes of Judges 4 are set up, we can
see these characteristics at work. The first scene after the introduction is short and marked by a summary time sense in which a long
time is portrayed or repeated or typical actions are described: "At
that time Deborah, a prophetess, wife of Lappidoth, was judging
Israel. She used to sit under the palm of Deborah between Ramah
and Bethel in the hill country of Ephraim; and the Israelites came
up to her for judgment" (Judg. 4:4–5). This scene introduces a new
character, Deborah, so it is clearly a new scene. However, the time
sense is spread over a long period as Deborah's leadership is described. When the time sense changes to more immediate action
and a new character is introduced, a new scene starts, even though
the NRSV does not begin a new paragraph here: "She sent and summoned Barak . . ." (4:6). The next three and a half verses describe
a scene where Deborah summons Barak and they engage in a dialogue in which she instructs him to lead some of the Israelite tribes
against King Jabin's army commander, Sisera, and his army. The

scene changes—once again mid-paragraph in the NRSV—when the time flow switches back to a more summary and long-range format. "Then Deborah got up and went with Barak to Kedesh. Barak summoned Zebulun and Naphtali to Kedesh; and ten thousand warriors went up behind him" (4:9–10). Here in one sentence some weeks must pass while Barak summons his militia. Yet within this single paragraph (4:4–10), we technically have three scenes that a movie director would have to stage, each in its own way: a summary of usual circumstances about Deborah, an active scene of dialogue that plans a particular battle, and another summary of longer-time action when the troops are gathered.

Another little summary scene follows in verse 11. This verse functions to give background about one of the tribes that was also in the area of the setting of the story, the Kenites, who apparently were not antagonistic to either the Israelites or the Canaanites in the battles of the time. We as readers do not know why this information is given to us at this point, but it will become clear later in the story. This foreshadowing is another technique used in typical biblical narratives, alerting readers to be aware that all information given by a story is likely to be significant in some way.

The main scene of the military engagement between Sisera and Barak occupies verses 12–16. Its beginning is signaled by a time change and a change in characters. "When Sisera was told that Barak son of Abinoam had gone up to Mount Tabor, Sisera called out all his chariots . . ." (4:12–13). The new scene begins by tracing the actions of the Canaanite commander. What follows is a scene that contains only one line of dialogue but much description of actions around the battle, which is won by Barak through the Lord's intervention. The outcome of the scene is that the army of Sisera is destroyed.

But the action of the story is not over, because we are told in the middle of the battle scene that Sisera, the commander of the Canaanite army, escaped from the battle by running away. So the next scene begins with another typical narrative opening: "Now Sisera had fled away on foot to the tent of Jael wife of Heber the

Kenite; for there was peace between King Jabin of Hazor and the clan of Heber the Kenite" (4:17). Three classic elements of biblical plots are at work here. First, the "now" at the start of the verse is one of the signals about a change of time and location that is used to start scenes. Second, the verse accomplishes what we might call the "meanwhile, back at the ranch" move. The previous scene mentioned Sisera running from the battle but went on to describe the end of the battle. Now the story resumes with what is happening to Sisera—the scene switches to follow his actions, which we have to assume have been going on while the battle was being waged. Finally, we now see why the little summary in verse 11 about the Kenites has been included—it sets the stage for Sisera thinking he might find a hiding place among this allied people.

It turns out in the story that Sisera's hope for escape among the Kenites is misplaced. Jael, the wife of the Kenites' leader, initially acts as Sisera expects and reassures him when she brings him into her tent. But Jael surprises both the reader and Sisera (though he does not live to realize it!) when she betrays his trust by killing him in his sleep. The scene contains dialogue between Sisera and Jael but ends abruptly with his end. The final scene of the story then is the summary in verse 23 that was quoted above—and now you can see how all the scenes of the story work to accomplish the plot and achieve the satisfactory ending that wraps up the action of the plot.

Plot Development: Story Arc

Judges 4 can also be used to illustrate the story line or story arc characteristic of plots, like the imaginary family story that we alluded to above. While employing this feature of narrative, biblical writing remains terse, but the plot conflict, complications, crisis, and resolution are present.

You can see these steps of a plot in Judges 4. The problem or conflict of this particular story is the threat to the Israelites posed by the Canaanite king and his army—that is the center of interest raised.

Will the Israelites be able to overcome this threat? All the action of the story works in one way or another to answer this question.

The calling and appointment of Barak by Deborah so that he will summon and lead a military force is a major step in forwarding the plot, a step that holds hope that the conflict of the plot will be positively resolved (at least from the Israelite point of view). However, another aspect of Barak's call works together with his military might to advance the plot.

Questions for Careful Readers

What is the problem or conflict driving the plot?

What complications are introduced as the plot is worked out?

Where is the crisis or turning point (or points)?

What happens in the resolution phase?

Are expectations that are set up by the story fulfilled, broken, changed?

[Deborah] said to him, "The LORD, the God of Israel, commands you, 'Go, take position at Mount Tabor, bringing ten thousand from the tribe of Naphtali and the tribe of Zebulun. I will draw out Sisera, the general of Jabin's army, to meet you by the Wadi Kishon with his chariots and his troops; and I will give him into your hand.'" (Judg. 4:6–7)

In the working out of the plot conflict, Deborah and Barak have another ally: the Lord, the God of Israel, who, as Barak learns through the word of the prophetess Deborah, is actually the one behind the action in the story. God's help in the battle will be decisive, as we see when the battle scene itself happens, and Deborah assures Barak, "Up! For this is the day on which the LORD has given Sisera into your hand. The LORD is indeed going out before you" (4:14). The effectiveness of God's help is stated just two verses later: "All the army of Sisera fell by the sword; no one was left" (4:16).

If this had been a simple story with only one scene that functions to bring the conflict to its crisis point, the scene in verses 12–16 would have accomplished that. The problem of the plot, the threat of the Canaanite army, is apparently resolved and the story could end here. However, this plot adds a complication to the story arc, which is a twist or additional element that leaves the original conflict open. This complication is first signaled in the story in the call scene when Deborah appoints Barak. Barak asks Deborah to accompany him into battle: Deborah responds that she will go with him, but adds a caution: "I will surely go with you; nevertheless, the road on which you are going will not lead to your glory, for the LORD will sell Sisera into the hand of a woman" (4:9).

The story will need to resolve this mystery to be complete, so the big battle scene cannot be the full account. In the scenes of the story arc that work out the plot, the complication is presented when Sisera flees the battle scene. Clearly, if the army commander is still at large, the threat is not over, so the story continues to hold interest—it is not complete yet. It takes another scene to bring the story to its ultimate crisis point, when both the mystery of an enemy army commander being killed by a woman and the complication of Sisera fleeing the battle come to a crisis point. Jael aids the Israelites by cleverly tricking Sisera and then killing him. Only with that action are all the lines of the story plot completed—thus it is the principal turning point of the story. Now the Israelites are truly safe from the immediate threat, the mystery of how a woman might kill an army commander is solved, and Sisera's escape is resolved.

A further resolution is added in summary form—namely, that eventually the Israelites conquer the king of Hazor (4:23). This summary illustrates another typical element of biblical narrative, answering the question of whether the expectations in the story are fulfilled, broken, or changed. In this case, we have the full confirmation that the expectations are fulfilled.

However, sometimes the expectations set up by the original problem or crisis of the plot are changed during the story line—unexpected events happen that alter the expected outcome. This is similar to a modern crime scene investigation drama that unexpectedly turns up quite a different perpetrator of the murder than anticipated, although biblical narrative usually offers less dramatic outcomes, even when the expectations are changed.

The way this change in plot expectations can work is evident in a story like 2 Kings 5. This one is in a series of stories about the prophet Elisha, who interacts with both peasants and kings. Throughout the narratives, the northern kingdom of Israel is shown to be sometimes threatened by the neighboring kingdom of Aram. Particularly in chapter 5, Naaman is the commander of the army of Aram, and he has leprosy and is seeking a cure. The problem of the story would seem to focus on whether and how Naaman can be cured, but as an army commander of a sometimes enemy of Israel, there would not be high expectations for any help from that quarter. However, a captive Israelite slave girl in Naaman's household tells him about a prophet in Samaria, the capital of Israel, who she says can cure him. Now the expectations do center on Israel and its prophet, but still questions linger—will a prophet from an enemy country really want or be able to cure him?

The story line tells of Naaman's journey to Samaria armed with a letter from his own king to the king of Israel authorizing a cure. When the Israelite king despairs of being able to accomplish such a task, Elisha hears about the situation and asks that Naaman come to him, setting the issue in terms of his own authority and power: "Let him come to me, that he may learn that there is a prophet in Israel" (5:8). When Naaman travels to Elisha's house, the prophet refuses to see him and merely sends out a message that the foreigner should wash himself seven times in the Jordan River to be cured. Initially angry at Elisha's unwillingness to perform the cure himself, Naaman is convinced by his servants to do as Elisha has commanded. "So he went down and immersed himself seven times in the Jordan, according to the word of the man of God; his flesh was restored like the flesh of a young boy, and he was clean" (5:14).

For an enemy army commander to be cured by the power of a god of another country speaking through a prophet is unexpected, so the story certainly grabs the reader's attention. And the story goes on to bend expectations even more. Naaman returns to Elisha to give witness. "Then he returned to the man of God, he and all his company; he came and stood before him and said, 'Now I know that there is no God in all the earth except in Israel'" (5:15). As the story resolves, Naaman states that when he returns to Aram, he will from now on worship only the Lord of Israel through sacrifices, and he asks for Elisha to issue a pardon for him when he has to accompany his master the king of Aram in worship to the god of Aram. Elisha grants his request with the words "Go in peace" (5:19).

The plot question about whether this foreign army commander can be cured has been resolved. The simple hope for a cure has been fulfilled, though by an unexpected source, an Israelite prophet. Beyond that, the foreign commander has come to recognize the power of the God of Israel and returns to his own country as a worshiper. The plot line has carried the anticipation of the story well beyond usual or simplistic fulfillments, to bend the expectations both of the story and about the willingness and power of Israel's God and prophet to work with outsiders to the Israelite community.

Plot Development: Sequences

Another characteristic of biblical narrative plots is the use of particular types of sequences that structure the events of a story line and involve significant repetition. These sequences are called a "command-enactment-report" sequence and a "forecast-enactment-report" sequence. Basically, a particular character issues a command (like a king) or a forecast (like a prophet). Sometimes the originating statement is an inquiry, challenge, or quest—for example, a king inquires of a seer about the outcome of a particular war plan. The story arc then follows what happens when the command, forecast, or inquiry is acted upon by other characters, which often involves several scenes and in some cases a number of chapters of text. The story arc wraps up either when a report is brought back to the original issuer of the command/forecast/inquiry about what happened to their statement or when the storyteller confirms the result in a summary. These sequences use a lot of repetition because often the originating statement is repeated each time some action affects its outcome, and then again when the report is given that wraps up the action.

The amount of repetition can make such stories difficult for modern readers, since contemporary usage tries to avoid repetition.

However, you may already be familiar with such a plot structure, as popular tales often use it. A king in a fairy tale, for example, may issue a challenge that the knight who can slay the fearsome dragon will receive a treasure of gold. Three different knights try, and each time the knight fails, but the words of the challenge are repeated exactly with each attempt. Then perhaps an unexpected character attempts the task—a clever peasant or bright serving woman outsmarts the dragon. When the report is brought back to the king, the challenge is repeated again, only this time the new information that a surprising character has saved the kingdom is incorporated into the repetition. The king, to keep the spirit of his original challenge, rewards the successful dragon slayer with the gold.

Questions for Careful Readers

Does repetition occur at any level within the story—words, phrases, events, scenes?

Are there any "command-enactment-report" sequences or "forecast-enactment-report" sequences in the narrative?

If so, does the repeated element confirm, change, contradict, or comment on the previous speech/event/element?

We can see a brilliant use of a sequence structure of a plot at work in 2 Kings 1 (again, it would be helpful to read the whole story as it will be only excerpted here). This story interweaves two conflicting sequences, one issued by a king and one by a prophet; this heightens the conflict of the story, the question of whose statement will be the outcome of the story arc. The story begins with the information that King Ahaziah of Israel has been injured in a fall at the palace and has issued an inquiry by messengers to a god of a neighboring kingdom, asking for a divine word on whether he will recover. At that moment, the word of the Lord God of Israel comes by a messenger (a better translation than "angel") to Elijah, sending him to challenge the king on why he must seek the word of a foreign god and to announce that the king will die of his injuries. So the conflict of the plot is set in this clash of royal word against prophetic word: who is the real God in this story, the foreign god or the God of Israel, and whose word about the king's fate will prove true?

The story line relates the initial results of the king's inquiry when the messengers sent to inquire of the foreign god return to say the following, which repeats the divine word that Elijah received:

> There came a man to meet us, who said to us, "Go back to the king who sent you, and say to him: Thus says the LORD: Is it because there is no God in Israel that you are sending to inquire of Baal-zebub, the god of Ekron? Therefore you shall not leave the bed to which you have gone, but shall surely die." (2 Kings 1:6)

By the messengers' description of the man as "a hairy man, with a leather belt around his waist," the king recognizes Elijah (1:8). In response to Elijah's divine word about the king's death, the king then sends a command directly to Elijah to come before him. At this point the plot continues to play off the conflict between the king's command and Elijah's prophecy.

Three quick scenes follow; in each scene the king sends a captain and fifty men to Elijah (who is sitting on a hilltop), commanding his presence. The first statement of the king's command is simple: "O man of God, the king says, 'Come down'" (1:9). In response Elijah ups the ante and identifies the real issue about divine power. The results are immediate: "Elijah answered the captain of fifty, 'If I am a man of God, let fire come down from heaven and consume you and your fifty.' Then fire came down from heaven, and consumed him and his fifty" (1:10).

When the second captain sent by the king repeats the summons, we have an example of how repetition can intensify the message: "O man of God, this is the king's order: Come down quickly!" (1:11). However, the second captain receives exactly the same deadly response and result from Elijah as the first captain; here the story uses almost exact repetition, intensifying the point by adding only that the fire comes from God. In both these instances of repetition, the story arc reinforces the conflict between the king's command and the prophet's word.

The third captain sent by the king has apparently learned a lesson from the repetition of fate of the first two and tries a different approach: "So the third captain of fifty went up, and came and fell on his knees before Elijah, and entreated him, 'O man of God, please let my life, and the life of these fifty servants of yours, be precious in your sight'" (2 Kings 1:13).

After the speech by this third captain, Elijah receives another word from the Lord, that he should go to the king, and he does so. The pattern of the fate of the first two royal captains is broken. While the king has now gotten Elijah's positive response to his command, the story arc is not done with the main question of the story: who is the real God in this story, the foreign god or the God of Israel, and whose word about the king's fate will prove true? The story moves immediately to what Elijah says to the king, when he repeats God's word directly to Ahaziah. This third, almost verbatim repetition adds force to the prophetic word: "Thus says the LORD: Because you have sent messengers to inquire of Baal-zebub, the god of Ekron,—is it because there is no God in Israel to inquire of his word?—therefore you shall not leave the bed to which you have gone, but you shall surely die" (2 Kings 1:16).

The final verse quickly communicates the outcome of the conflict between the king's command and the prophet's word, settles the question of which god is more powerful, reports the king's fate, and neatly repeats the point that Elijah originally made to the king: "So he died according to the word of the LORD that Elijah had spoken" (2 Kings 1:17).

Characterization

In literature from all ages, the portraits drawn of the characters that inhabit a story are often dramatic and memorable. Readers and audiences can remember the wonderful details of a strongly portrayed character in a book or movie—the surly or dangerous villain, the smart and sharp heroine, the leading man with eyes that speak of hidden depths. Characters, even fictional ones, may inspire audiences to do anything from imitating their admirable actions in their own lives to dressing up in costumes for science fiction conventions. Modern novels and stories often illustrate a character by full description, using words to depict the person's physical characteristics, background, likes and dislikes, and inner thoughts and emotions. Movies portray characters visually and in the words of other characters but also use voice-overs to include the visually hidden inner life of a character.

Biblical historical narrative has its own typical ways of portraying characters; some ways are transparent to a modern reader, and others are more subtle and so need some introduction. One of the perhaps tricky parts of biblical characterization is that the audience is rarely given an outright description of a character's appearance, background, or thoughts. However, biblical stories do have other ways of conveying what the people in the stories are like, including characterization that could be described using the old saying "Actions speak louder than words."

Characterization: Direct Description

Question for Careful Readers

What direct description of characters is given by the narrator?

We will start with just a few examples of direct description of characters.

We have to include a caution, however, that this is not the usual method of portrayal that biblical narrative uses. However, since it is a relatively rare technique, it is worth noticing when direct description is used. For an initial example, Saul, the first king of the tribes when Israel was moving toward monarchy, is introduced with the following words: "There was a man of Benjamin whose name was Kish son of Abiel . . . , a man of wealth. He had a son whose name was Saul, a handsome young man. There was not a man among the people of Israel more handsome than he; he stood head and shoulders above everyone else" (1 Sam. 9:1–2).

We learn quite a bit about Saul here—his place of origin, his pedigree in his family lineage (mostly omitted here for brevity), his name, his family's wealth, and his striking physical appearance that literally puts him "head and shoulders above" every other character.

The initial impression given in this detail about the character of Saul is that he apparently is worthy to be a leader—at least as far as background and physical appearance can tell us. The question this leaves the reader with, however, is whether he will turn out to be the leader and king that seems promised by this description. And that is the stuff of the plot that follows in the next seven chapters, in which Saul's royal leadership is depicted as falling far short of this promising appearance.

But does physical attractiveness always spell trouble? In another story about the period of the emergence of the monarchy in Israel, we meet two people whose descriptions do predict their true character and actions. During the time when David and Saul are rivals for the kingship, David is an outlaw taking refuge from Saul's rage in the wilderness of southern Judah. He meets up with a husband and wife who are described in this way: "There was a man in Maon, whose property was in Carmel. The man was very rich; he had three thousand sheep and a thousand goats. . . . Now the name of the man was Nabal, and the name of his wife Abigail. The woman was clever and beautiful, but the man was surly and mean" (1 Sam. 25:2–3).

As this story plays out, both Nabal and Abigail are revealed as true to their depiction in this introduction. Nabal refuses to support David and gives him a hard time; Abigail acts as peacemaker, bringing food for David's men and insightful words about David's future as a leader. As the story ends, both seem to get "what they deserve" when Nabal dies after a drunken binge and Abigail eventually becomes one of David's wives. These examples from 1 Samuel illustrate the types of direct description you will find on occasion in the texts and what to watch for in the actions that follow the character descriptions.

Characterization: By Actions

One of the principal ways that biblical narrative portrays characters is by the actions of the characters that are a part of the story. This is a less direct way of gaining access to character portrayal, but it is

Characterization in History Writing: Biblical and Modern

Characterization in biblical writing rarely relies on direct description by the narrator and rarely gives information about a character's internal state of mind or thoughts. Excerpts below from the description of David show some of the very few verses (from forty-two chapters in David's story) where he is directly described by the narrator or where his internal thoughts or emotions are described, in comparison with excerpts about John Adams from a modern history book,[a] where direct descriptions of him and his internal thoughts and feelings are regularly included.

Biblical: David	Modern: John Adams
Direct description: "Now he was ruddy, and had beautiful eyes, and was handsome" (1 Sam. 16:12).	Direct description: "The chin was firm, the nose sharp, almost birdlike. But it was the dark, perfectly arched brows and keen blue eyes that gave the face its vitality" (18).
Direct description: "Now David was the son of an Ephrathite of Bethlehem in Judah" (1 Sam. 17:12).	Direct description: "As his family and friends knew, Adams was both a devout Christian and an independent thinker, and he saw no conflict in that. He was hard-headed and a man of 'sensibility,' a close observer of human folly as displayed in everyday life and fired by an inexhaustible love of books and scholarly reflection" (19).
Internal view: "David . . . was very much afraid of King Achish of Gath" (1 Sam. 21:12).	Internal view: "That he relished the sharp conflict and theater of the courtroom, that he loved the esteem that came with public life, no less than he loved 'my farm, my family and goose quill [pen],' there is no doubt, however frequently he protested to the contrary" (19–20).
Internal view: "David said in his heart, 'I shall now perish one day by the hand of Saul'" (1 Sam. 27:1).	Internal view: "The grand houses and hospitality [when he was in New York City] were such as Adams had never known, even if, as a self-respecting New Englander, he thought New Yorkers lacking in decorum" (24–25).
Internal view: [After his son Absalom's death:] "The king was deeply moved . . . and wept" (2 Sam. 18:33).	Internal view: [As a young man, thinking about his future:] "Increasingly, however, the subject uppermost in mind was himself, as waves of loneliness, feelings of abject discontent over his circumstances, dissatisfaction with his own nature, seemed at times nearly to overwhelm him" (41).

a. David McCullough, *John Adams* (New York: Simon and Schuster, 2001).

often used in the sparse style of biblical narrative art, which prefers actions over long descriptions of a person. Actions in biblical stories do speak louder than words (although we will see in the next section that words in the form of dialogue by the characters also add to our knowledge about them). In modern novels and especially movies there is a type of lead character known as an "action hero"—this type of character is better described by what they *do* than by how they are directly described by the storyteller. Of course, as soon as we focus on actions used in portraying characterization, there is an overlap with plot, so that much of what you learned in the previous sections will hold true.

We can return to the character of Abigail in 1 Samuel 25 to see a portrayal by actions. The plot of the story revolves around David's request to Nabal for food during a local feast for David's men who have provided protection for Nabal's herds in the wilderness areas. When Nabal rudely refuses to help, David takes offense and swears an oath that Nabal will pay for the insult by David's bloody vengeance. Abigail learns from a worried servant that her mean-spirited husband has refused to support David with food and that this will lead to evil against all her household (25:17). She immediately takes matters into her own hands to deal with the threatened violence.

> **Questions for Careful Readers**
>
> How do actions by characters aid in their characterization?
>
> Do the actions give a depiction of the type of person?

> Then Abigail hurried and took two hundred loaves, two skins of wine, five sheep ready dressed, five measures of parched grain, one hundred clusters of raisins, and two hundred cakes of figs. She loaded them on donkeys and said to her young men, "Go on ahead of me; I am coming after you." But she did not tell her husband Nabal. As she rode on the donkey and came down under cover of the mountain, David and his men came down toward her; and she met them. . . . When Abigail saw David, she hurried and alighted from the donkey, and fell before David on her face, bowing to the ground. (1 Sam. 25:18–20, 23)

Without any direct description of Abigail as a person, this text paints a vivid picture of her. She is quick-witted and resourceful, fearless, keenly aware of the potential outcomes and politics of the situation, well organized, authoritative, and able to command the resources and people of her large household without any input from her husband. She single-handedly averts the threat by offering the requested feast to David and in her ability to be both strong and humble turns David's anger aside from her household.

Actions by a character can also be used by the biblical text to convey a less complimentary characterization. Sometimes this happens by what characters do and other times by what they fail to do. In 1 Samuel 3, Eli is the old priest in charge of the sanctuary. Again, this story is set in the early days of the transition to monarchy when the ark of God that was the center of worship for the tribes was tended by priests at a local sanctuary in the hill country. When this story occurs the text has already related that Eli has lost control over his sons, who have turned to extorting sacrificial food from the people rather than serving as legitimate worship leaders as expected of a priest's sons. So Eli's own leadership as a priest is already questionable. In the story in chapter 3, a young boy named Samuel is serving as the assistant to Eli.

> At that time Eli, whose eyesight had begun to grow dim so that he could not see, was lying down in his room; the lamp of God had not yet gone out, and Samuel was lying down in the temple of the LORD, where the ark of God was. Then the LORD called, "Samuel! Samuel!" and he said, "Here I am!" and ran to Eli, and said, "Here I am, for you called me." But he said, "I did not call; lie down again." So he went and lay down. (1 Sam. 3:2–5)

The story previously related that "the word of the LORD was rare in those days; visions were not widespread" (3:1). It seems this call to Samuel from the Lord is unusual. However, the setting is the sanctuary, where God would be present if anywhere. Now, the text tells us directly that "the word of the LORD had not yet been revealed" to Samuel (3:7), so there is no expectation that he would perceive what is happening. However, one could assume that the priest in charge of the sanctuary might have a greater sensitivity to God's will and presence.

After the Lord's first call to Samuel, the story goes on to repeat this incident two more times. The second time, like the first, Eli is without insight or curiosity and simply sends Samuel back to bed. The third time, something finally clicks for the old priest. "The LORD called Samuel again, a third time. And he got up and went to Eli, and said, 'Here I am, for you called me.' Then Eli perceived that the LORD was calling the boy. Therefore Eli said to Samuel, 'Go, lie down; and if he calls you, you shall say, "Speak, LORD, for your servant is listening"'" (1 Sam. 3:8–9). Finally the priest perceives that this call in the night might be something from God to which Samuel should pay attention, and he gives the instructions to the boy that are the appropriate response in call stories. This is a subtle turn of characterization, dependent on Eli's portrayal as slow-witted and lacking in insight. Eli's lack of action creates a question: should an experienced priest not be able to perceive more quickly that the Lord might call someone at the sanctuary? Once the question is raised, it adds to the accumulating evidence of Eli's lack of leadership.

Characterization: By Dialogue

A character's words also add to the way that character is portrayed in biblical historical narrative. The storyteller uses dialogue in biblical narratives to reveal what the speakers are like, as well as having the characters initiate, reflect on, and react to incidents in the plot—all of which adds to characterization. In modern television shows and movies, much effort goes into the dialogue by the script writers because that oral medium will convey a lot of their story. In a similar way, dialogue carries much of the information a text gives about the people in the story.

We will use the story in Nehemiah 5 to illustrate how dialogue can give a window into a character. All the "action" in this story happens through dialogue. The story has previously related that

Questions
for Careful Readers

How does dialogue add to
  the characterization of the
  main characters?

Who speaks in the story?
  Who does not speak?

Are a character's words reliable, confirmed by others,
  by the narrator, by events?

Nehemiah has been appointed governor of the postexilic Jewish community by the Persian emperor to restore the wall of the city of Jerusalem. Other problems and struggles of the community also come to him, as in this story where Nehemiah receives a report about the difficult economic situation of some of the population. He hears that the poorest are being forced into debt to support their families, having to pledge their families as collateral on survival loans and in some cases sell their children into debt slavery to their richer Jewish neighbors in order to survive (5:2–5). Nehemiah learns all this in the story by means of anonymous quotes:

> And there were those who said, "We are having to borrow money on our fields and vineyards to pay the king's tax. Now our flesh is the same as that of our kindred; our children are the same as their children; and yet we are forcing our sons and daughters to be slaves, and some of our daughters have been ravished; we are powerless, and our fields and vineyards now belong to others." (Neh. 5:4–5)

The use of quotes here illustrates the effectiveness of dialogue—when the words of those who suffer are heard, the depth of their plight is communicated more forcefully than if a dispassionate description were given.

Nehemiah's response is also communicated in dialogue, in the first-person style of this part of the book of Nehemiah.

> I brought charges against the nobles and the officials; I said to them, "You are all taking interest from your own people." And I called a great assembly to deal with them, and said to them, "As far as we were able, we have bought back our Jewish kindred who had been sold to other nations; but now you are selling your own kin. . . !" They were silent, and could not find a word to say. . . . [So I said,] "Restore to them, this very day, their fields, their vineyards, their olive orchards, and their houses, and the interest on money, grain, wine, and oil

that you have been exacting from them." Then they said, "We will restore everything and demand nothing more from them. We will do as you say." . . . And all the assembly said, "Amen," and praised the LORD. And the people did as they had promised. (Neh. 5:7–8, 11–13)

In this exchange, the dialogue communicates a lot about the governor: he is direct, angry, and authoritative. He is portrayed as deeply concerned that the elite of the community have taken advantage of the poorer people for their own gain. He is knowledgeable about the greedy economic behavior of the rich and its effects on the poor. The inability of the rich to respond at first to his accusation is an illustration of how a failure to say something is part of characterization. Then in a quote, the elite assent to end their exploitation of the weaker members of the society, which will entail a financial loss for them. Thus these elements of the dialogue convey Nehemiah as powerful and effective—the success of his words is communicated by both the speechlessness of the rich and their assent. The final verse of the excerpt adds confirmation, in the style characteristic of biblical narrative. Yes, indeed, the narrator reports, the people did as they had promised.

One form of speaking by characters in biblical historical narratives is what we would call a monologue—where one character speaks for a length of time. In the historical books, such extended words from one character include formats like speeches, prayers, psalms, and farewell addresses, sometimes in regular declarative sentences and sometimes in poetry. These forms are used to good effect to advance the plot and to develop the characterization of the person speaking. All the books we are examining include speeches, prayers, or psalms by leading characters, such as Joshua, Deborah, Hannah, Samuel, David, and Solomon. In the books of Chronicles, Ezra, and Nehemiah, there are speeches from David, Solomon, and various Judahite kings and from both Ezra and Nehemiah. David leads the pack in most monologues included, as would be fitting for the most famous of Judah's kings.

We can see how a speech as a form of dialogue conveys information about a character by looking at King Abijah's speech in 2 Chronicles

13. The story has just told of the split in the kingdom when Jeroboam rebelled against Solomon's heir in Judah, Rehoboam, and took the northern tribes into their own state. Rehoboam's heir, Abijah, is faced with a war against Israel under Jeroboam. Abijah musters his forces, four hundred units of warriors, against Jeroboam's eight hundred military units. Though Abijah's forces are outnumbered, Abijah's speech reveals his character and commitment, as he challenges his enemy.

> Then Abijah stood . . . and said, "Listen to me, Jeroboam and all Israel! Do you not know that the LORD God of Israel gave the kingship over Israel forever to David and his sons . . . ? Yet Jeroboam son of Nebat, a servant of Solomon son of David, rose up and rebelled against his lord. . . . And now you think that you can withstand the kingdom of the LORD in the hand of the sons of David. . . . Have you not driven out the priests of the LORD . . . and made priests for yourselves like the peoples of other lands? . . . But as for us, the LORD is our God, and we have not abandoned him. We have priests ministering to the LORD who are descendants of Aaron, and Levites for their service. . . . See, God is with us at our head. . . . O Israelites, do not fight against the LORD, the God of your ancestors; for you cannot succeed." (2 Chron. 13:4–6, 8–10, 12)

Abijah speaks confidently of the Davidic dynasty's divine legitimacy on the throne in Judah. He mocks the power and authenticity of Jeroboam, trying to undermine his rival's legitimacy. He questions the religious purity of the northern state, accusing them of rejecting the true priests of the Lord. He claims that Judah is true to the Lord and that Judah's priesthood can trace its lineage back to Aaron, the priestly brother of Moses himself. He goes so far as to call to the Israelites to give up the battle—they cannot win. These words speak of a king who is supremely confident in his faith in the God who has placed his dynastic house on the throne. He is bold, mocking his rival and the motley priesthood on which his rival depends. In the events following this speech, Abijah's words are confirmed by events. "God defeated Jeroboam and all Israel before Abijah and Judah" (13:15). In this characterization of Abijah through the words

Dialogue: Famous Movie Quotes

Dialogue plays an important part in modern novels, movies, and stories. As in ancient storytelling, dialogue in modern storytelling conveys plot action and characterization. Here are some famous lines of dialogue from movies that have entered the shared consciousness of North American culture.[a] These one-liners capture a critical moment in the plot of a movie or portray a dramatic element of a character's personality.

Frankly, my dear, I don't give a damn.	*Gone with the Wind*, 1939
Toto, I've got a feeling we're not in Kansas anymore.	*The Wizard of Oz*, 1939
Round up the usual suspects.	*Casablanca*, 1942
Bond. James Bond.	*Dr. No*, 1962
Open the pod bay doors please, HAL.	*2001: A Space Odyssey*, 1968
May the Force be with you.	*Star Wars*, 1977
Go ahead, make my day.	*Sudden Impact*, 1983
Houston, we have a problem.	*Apollo 13*, 1995
I'm the king of the world!	*Titanic*, 1997
My precious.	*The Lord of the Rings: The Two Towers*, 2002

a. "AFI's 100 Years . . . 100 Movie Quotes," *Wikipedia*, accessed December 29, 2012, http://en.wikipedia.org/wiki/AFI%27s_100_Years...100_Movie_Quotes.

of his speech, we see how an extended monologue reveals insight into a character. The confirmation of Abijah's words in the report of the battle is also a typical element of how both dialogue and plot work in biblical narrative.

Point of View

Point of view is an element in all kinds of stories, whether in written form, like a book, or in visual form, like a movie. At its most basic, point of view is the perspective from which the reader or viewer is seeing the action. For example, in a television show, the camera usually acts as a "neutral observer," standing outside the action of each scene to show the viewer what is happening in the scene and what each character is doing. In a story, this is called "third-person narration," where the characters are talked about as "they," "he," or "she" and the action is related from the viewpoint of someone standing just outside the scene. However, the camera in a movie shoot or the plot in a novel might also follow the actions and words of some characters more than others—so, for example, the audience might see what the earth forces are planning to do in fighting off the aliens but never see what the aliens are planning. Other dramas and novels might show what both sides are doing; this heightens the tension, particularly in crime stories and mysteries, where the whole plot revolves around figuring out "whodunit." There is another possible point of view, however, which is where the camera in a sense sees through the eyes of a particular character—showing you what that person is seeing in a scene, conveying a very particular point of view from one character. The same inside point of view might be conveyed in a movie or book when the inner thoughts or emotions of a particular character are included, as a voice-over in a movie or as an inner dialogue in a story.

Biblical narrative has parallel elements for each of these types of point of view. However, by far the most common point of view in biblical stories is that of the outside observer, the third-person narrator who can report on the whole plot and characters. The storyteller in biblical narrative is all-knowing, that is, the narrator knows and can relate what each person is doing, thinking, and feeling; how every action is happening in the plot; and how the whole story will turn out. However, just because the storyteller takes a point of view that could report on the actions, words, and inner thoughts of every character does not mean the storyteller always gives that much information. As noted at the start of this chapter, biblical narrative is often restrained, giving only enough description to convey the essentials of the story and its characters. Thus while the narrative most often relates what any outside observer might see, on occasion the story will give a different perspective.

A brief scene from 1 Samuel 18 in the story of David's rise to power will illustrate two aspects of point of view. The narration leading up to this scene has related that while Saul is on the throne, David has been selected and anointed as the new king by the Lord, who was acting through the prophet Samuel. David has gone on to enjoy huge success on the battlefield, killing the giant Philistine warrior, Goliath.

Questions for Careful Readers

Through whose eyes are we seeing each scene?

Within an all-knowing narrator's viewpoint, do we see any other points of view?

Do we hear the inner thoughts of any character?

Is the point of view of any character consistently denied to the reader?

> As they were coming home, when David returned from killing the Philistine, the women came out of all the towns of Israel, singing and dancing. . . . And the women sang, . . . "Saul has killed his thousands, and David his ten thousands." Saul was very angry, for this saying displeased him. He said, "They have ascribed to David ten thousands, and to me they have ascribed thousands; what more can he have but the kingdom?" (1 Sam. 18:6–8)

In this scene, we are given an interior view of Saul's emotions as he sees David's popularity and of Saul's fear that he will lose the throne. By contrast, there is no interior view of David himself—he is opaque to the reader. This illustrates both possibilities of viewpoint—an interior one and one that completely denies any interior knowledge.

Another scene can illustrate the technique that switches points of view between the perspectives seen by two characters. In 2 Kings 9, the narrative relates that the prophet Elisha gives the Lord's word that the current evil king of Israel will be removed from the throne. The prophetically anointed usurper, an army commander named Jehu, takes over the throne, murdering his king and grabbing power. As the coup continues, Jehu must also kill the powerful queen mother Jezebel, who has already been characterized in the ongoing story as evil and cunning. The death scene takes place in a fortified city where the queen mother has held power. As you read this scene, imagine how you might film it—where would the camera stand for each verse?

> When Jehu came to Jezreel, Jezebel heard of it; she painted her eyes, and adorned her head, and looked out of the window. As Jehu entered the gate, she said, "Is it peace, . . . murderer of your master?" He looked up to the window and said, "Who is on my side? Who?" Two or three eunuchs looked out at him. He said, "Throw her down." So they threw her down; some of her blood spattered on the wall and on the horses, which trampled on her. (2 Kings 9:30–33)

The scene starts from Jezebel's perspective in the upper room where she prepares as royalty to meet her fate. The camera angle when she looks out the window might show the scene as she sees it—looking down on the courtyard below as the new king enters the gate of the city. Then the scene switches to Jehu's perspective, and the camera might follow. From Jehu's location in the courtyard below, the camera might look up toward Jezebel in the window as he calls out to force the servants attending Jezebel to choose sides—his as the new king, or hers as the old queen mother. The eunuchs make their allegiance known as the camera angle quickly switches back to Jezebel's window—they throw her out. The final quick switch comes as the camera returns to the courtyard to view the bloody scene of her death. This is a particularly dramatic scene that illustrates different views on a scene, with quick movements of the "camera's eye."

Time Flow

The final brief category of narrative art that helps to build an intriguing narrative is the use of time in relating the story. You are familiar with different senses of time from movies or novels: the normal flow of time during a conversation, the quick jump forward to a new scene several years ahead, or the excruciatingly slow ticking of the clock as the detective disarms the bomb. As noted in the section above on "Scenic Structures," most often in biblical narrative

time flows in a normal forward direction, because most often events are told
in chronological order. However, other
timing relationships between scenes are
possible, and this brief section will review the possibilities so that you can
recognize them as you read.

> **Questions
> for Careful Readers**
>
> How are events related in the
> sequencing of the story?
>
> Are there indications of simulta-
> neous events, use of the past,
> or indications of the future?
>
> Where does time move slowly
> or quickly in the story?
>
> Does time jump in transitions
> between scenes?[2]

Even when time flows in a forward
direction in narrative, variety is possible. Sometimes one scene will follow
another with a sense of immediacy, with
no gap in time, as when two new charac-
ters enter the same location that two other characters have just left.
By contrast, a lot of time can pass in a very brief statement, when
the story uses a summary format to cover a significant amount of
time. For example, in the narrative relating the reign of King Asa
in Judah, just after a fairly detailed description of a battle against
one enemy and a renewal of the covenant with God back in Jerusalem, the story includes this verse: "And there was no more war
until the thirty-fifth year of the reign of Asa" (2 Chron. 15:19). In
these few words, many years pass; the next scene in the king's reign
takes place in his thirty-sixth year on the throne. Or, a shorter but
specified amount of time might pass between scenes, as in the story
that relates the movements of the ark of God before it was brought
to the temple in Jerusalem. "The ark of the LORD remained in the
house of Obed-edom the Gittite for three months" (2 Sam. 6:11).

Time moving in a forward direction can also move very slowly so
that the story makes it possible for the audience to pay particular
attention to what is happening. Any time there is dialogue or detail
about a person, object, or event given in a narrative, the timing of
the story slows down. Both of these story elements take up narrative
time and slow the pace of events. However, a story can also slow its

2. The "Questions for Careful Readers" in this chapter first appeared in Patricia
Dutcher-Walls, *Jezebel: Portraits of a Queen* (Collegeville, MN: Liturgical Press,
2004), 5, 8, 11, 12, and 14.

pace by repeating actions or events. In the story of Gideon, one of the deliverers of Israel in the era of the judges, all three techniques are used to make the narrative of the call of Gideon to leadership a long, slow story. Relating call narrative can be very efficient: God's messenger appears and issues the call to leadership, and the selected leader responds positively and immediately. However, Gideon takes most of a chapter to respond to the message, twice refusing to believe that the Lord's messenger could possibly pick him. This second exchange is typical of Gideon's stall tactics: "Then the LORD turned to him and said, 'Go in this might of yours and deliver Israel from the hand of Midian; I hereby commission you.' He responded, 'But sir, how can I deliver Israel? My clan is the weakest in Manasseh, and I am the least in my family'" (Judg. 6:14–15). When Gideon finally starts to get it, he insists on preparing a meal for the divine messenger, which the story describes in great detail, further slowing the pace. Several more incidents take place before Gideon calls out the tribes to meet the enemy threat.

Biblical narrative uses several other time relationships on occasion. Sometimes a text needs to relate that two scenes have happened simultaneously. Obviously, a story cannot split a screen like a television or computer, so it has to relate events one at a time. We noted above how the Deborah story first relates one scene of the battle, then uses the word "now" to signal a new scene about Sisera's death that has a "meanwhile, back at the ranch" element to it. Biblical narrative can also move time forward or backward in a story, to relate a flashback or a jump ahead in time, sometimes as far ahead as the current time of the storyteller. This excerpt from the story of David's conquest of Jerusalem to be his capital city illustrates the typical narrative element of a forward notice in a story: "David took the stronghold of Zion, which is now the city of David" (2 Sam. 5:7). You can see how the storyteller jumps ahead to his own time to confirm the name of the city. This technique and all the ways we have reviewed about how the flow of time is noted in biblical historical narrative serve the purpose of helping to communicate the story being told, so that the audience has the satisfaction of a tale well told.

Conclusion

Stories are universal in all cultures of the world. Each culture or people has particular ways of telling a story. Understanding the storytelling art of a particular culture will enhance appreciation of its narratives. In particular, in order for a modern reader to see how the ancient storytelling of biblical narrative works, it is helpful to be aware of the conventions and techniques of ancient storytellers. The characteristics that we have reviewed in this chapter, including plot development, characterization, point of view, and timing, all combine to convey intriguing plot lines and animated characters. These carry the account of the past, but they also carry ideas, opinions, and viewpoints that are communicated through the story. The next chapter will explore how we can discern the interests of the text.

Suggested Reading

Alter, Robert. *The Art of Biblical Narrative*. New York: Basic Books, 1981.

Amit, Yairah. *Reading Biblical Narratives*. Minneapolis: Fortress, 2001.

Bar-Efrat, Shimon. *Narrative Art in the Bible*. Sheffield: Almond Press, 1989.

Gunn, David M. "Narrative Criticism." Pages 201–29 in *To Each Its Own Meaning*. Edited by Steven R. Haynes and Steven L. McKenzie. Revised and expanded edition. Louisville: Westminster John Knox, 1999.

Discussion Questions

1. How would you summarize the main differences between how stories were told in ancient Israel and how they are told today?

2. Using the story of David and Goliath (1 Sam. 17), imagine you are a movie director filming this story as closely as possible to the text itself. How many scenes would you need, and where

would each scene begin and end? How many actors (including extras) would you need in each scene? What advice would you give the actors playing David, Goliath, and Saul about how to play their parts to stay close to the text? What would be the timing of each scene—slow background or fast action? Would you need a narrator at any point to convey the story line?

3. Read one of the stories from the book of Kings (for example, 1 Kings 19:1–18). Try to find at least one example of each type of narrative technique described in this chapter.

3

Discerning the Interests of the Text

We have seen in the previous chapter how texts in the biblical historical books communicate in the form of stories. We have examined how biblical storytelling creates an engaging tale that conveys particulars about events and characters. Further, we have seen how storytelling holds an audience's attention, because the story generates interest. However, the biblical historical books also convey other information and ideas to their audiences in the form of opinions, evaluations, and points of view. It is probably clear in the reading you have done so far in excerpts from the biblical historical books that these texts express opinions and perspectives about the information they are relating. The stories are not neutral accounts or unbiased reports such as what we might expect from a form like an accident report that tries to give the facts of only a particular car accident. Rather, biblical reporting of incidents comes complete with various viewpoints that are communicated by the text. We will call this aspect of biblical history writing the "interests" of the text, and during the course of this chapter we will examine *how* the texts convey their interests, give a sampling of those interests, and see how these interests express the theology of the books.

In general, a text uses several types of techniques to get a reader's attention and make its points. When giving a speech, speakers might do something such as raise their voice or use dramatic whispers to get you to listen. When they really want to convince their audiences about an idea, they might quote an authority figure, cite a survey, or give a dramatic example of their point. If they want to persuade an audience *not* to do something, they might include a lot of negative examples about what might happen if that choice is made. All these kinds of persuasive techniques from a speech have corresponding techniques that written texts can use.

For any point or argument to be persuasive, speakers or writers must make that point present in the minds of their audience, so the broadest category of persuasive techniques are those that increase the presence of an idea in a speech or written text. A further category of techniques to convince an audience is the technique of drawing an association between something the audience already knows or agrees with and the outcome the speaker is seeking. In contrast, if writers want to discourage a reader from doing something, they might use techniques that cause a dissociation between an accepted idea and any temptation the reader might feel toward the discouraged action. All of these types of persuasive techniques have been studied by those who study rhetoric, the art of persuasion.[1] Learning to appreciate how a text makes its points clear and emphatic is a way of listening to the interests of those who wrote the texts.

The writing of the ancient authors of the Bible uses techniques like these to make points that were important to them and that they wanted their readers and hearers to appreciate. For this general introduction to how the historical writings of the Bible make their interests known, we will survey a number of practices without being too

1. Sources for this chapter include Yehoshua Gitay, "Rhetorical Criticism," in *To Each Its Own Meaning*, ed. Steven R. Haynes and Steven L. McKenzie (Louisville: Westminster John Knox, 1993), 135–49; Gerard Hauser, *Introduction to Rhetorical Theory* (Prospect Heights, IL: Waveland, 1991); Chaim Perelman, *The Realm of Rhetoric* (Notre Dame, IN: University of Notre Dame Press, 1982); Meir Sternberg, *The Poetics of Biblical Narrative: Ideological Literature and the Drama of Reading* (Bloomington: Indiana University Press, 1987); and Walter Brueggemann, *The Practice of Prophetic Imagination: Preaching an Emancipating Word* (Minneapolis: Fortress, 2012).

technical about the rhetorical specifics of ancient writing. However, one method of making a topic present to an audience is so characteristic of ancient writing that it is worth noting. This method is the use of repetition, either direct repetition of exact words or phrases or repetition of similar phrases, ideas, topics, and events. Usually writers of modern English are taught to avoid repetition because it seems boring or unoriginal. You might be able to remember a high school English teacher emphasizing that you needed to use a thesaurus in order to find synonyms to avoid repetition. Ancient teachers of rhetoric apparently taught just the opposite: how to use repetition in order to make a point emphatic. So we will include examining repetition as we learn about how ancient texts convey their interests.

Building Presence

Some of the most obvious methods for making an idea or point present in writing or speaking are simply to focus on it in various ways—emphasize it, keep repeating it, give a lot of detail about it, and assemble strong arguments in its support. Any idea or point that a person keeps coming back to reveals something about what that person is interested in. For example, if you wanted to know about the music tastes of a friend, you might take a look at his or her digital music library. Among the perhaps thousands of songs there, you might see many that are from the same group or from a small number of groups and singers. Or you might see a trend in the type of music—maybe you will come across a lot of classic rock or music by indie groups, or maybe your friend seems to gravitate toward jazz standards or new music.

When we look at the Old Testament, repetition is a common means for making something present in the text. There is one outstanding example of presence as a technique in the biblical historical

Questions for Careful Readers

What words, phrases, and ideas are brought forward by the ways the text makes them present to the reader?

What is emphasized by the text or across texts, particularly by the repetition of words, phrases, and ideas?

literature. The figure of David, the king who ruled over a united Israel and Judah, seems to be the single most present concept throughout the historical writing. In numerous stories we hear about the tales of his rise as a leader who becomes king, the intrigues and politics of his reign, the wars and victories of his time, and his decisions, as well as his mistakes. However, even beyond the actual stories about him and his time, his name and reputation dominate much of the rest of the history. Later stories keep referring to David as the most famous king of Israel and make him the standard against which other kings and leaders are judged.

Some statistics will make the point. In the books that include David's time and the history after that (from 1 Samuel on), there are 190 chapters. These chapters cover the history of about six hundred years. In sixty-one of those chapters we hear directly about the life and times of David. This means that about a third of the history that covers six hundred years is given over to telling about David—that is a lot of time spent on one king! When we look at David's legacy, we see how the later story is written to refer to him as a famous king and standard for other kings. There are mentions of David by name at least once in an additional sixty-two chapters of the historical books. Some of these chapters just briefly cite David as a king or mention the "city of David," a name for Jerusalem. However, other chapters mention him several times—one chapter from Solomon's reign refers to him sixteen times. This means that another third of the chapters of this six-hundred-year historical account mention David, making him a figure in a total of 65 percent of the history. This is a clear example of making something present in a body of literature. It should be evident that these texts are supremely interested in David as a role model and "leading man" and in invoking David's memory to convey the values and standards of the authors.

Establishing Authority

Often when speakers or writers want to make an argument stronger and more impressive, they will cite the opinions of experts and authorities to back up their own words. You have seen an "authority argument" at work every time an article, website, or speech quotes someone like a doctor, engineer, or other knowledgeable expert. Or statistics from a research group or think tank may be included to strengthen a point. The more known and respected the authority is, the better a quote works for the purposes of the speaker. You take advantage of an authority every time you look at a movie review before going to or downloading a movie—you are seeking a knowledgeable opinion about the movie, an evaluation that will help you decide whether it is worth watching. You have also experienced an authority argument if one of your parents ever closed a discussion with the line "Because I said so!"

Texts in the historical books of the Bible include many quotes from and references to authority figures. Of course, in the religious context of these texts, God is understood as the supreme authority in all matters, so any words from the Lord that are used support the point being made. Sometimes the stories report how God's words came by direct revelation. On some occasions, someone reports seeing God, though the traditions also caution that no one can see God and live (Exod. 33:20). More often the divine word is heard without a visual contact; seers relate how they have "heard" or "seen" the word of the Lord, or how a messenger from the Lord came to them, either directly or in a dream or vision. Other times God's words are reported by figures who are known to have a direct line to God's messages. Thus prophets in particular have an authority that is borrowed from God, so that they can be quoted passing on a message that comes from God's authority.

A prophetic story that underscores the authority of the prophets is Elijah's contest against the prophets of a rival god, Baal, set at the time when northern Israel was a relatively strong monarchy. In this

> **Questions for Careful Readers**
>
> What characters have authority in the story, or in what ways are certain figures made the focus of authority arguments so that they function with influence in subsequent chapters?
>
> How do characters then use their authority to affect or shape the actions and ideas of others?

story, each side of the prophetic rivalry sets up an offering and calls on its god to come down to light the burnt offering. The prophets of Baal call out, raving on, but no fire comes to light their offering. Elijah, the prophet of the Lord, then prays.

> The prophet Elijah . . . said, "O Lord, God of Abraham, Isaac, and Israel, let it be known this day that you are God in Israel, that I am your servant, and that I have done all these things at your bidding. Answer me, O Lord, answer me, so that this people may know that you, O Lord, are God. . . ." Then the fire of the Lord fell and consumed the burnt offering. (1 Kings 18:36–38)

The fire confirms the power of the Lord, but it also confirms the authority of the Lord's prophet, who is shown to have a true connection to God and to be able to speak in God's name and with God's power.

Other characters in the historical books also have authority because of their social or political position. Kings inevitably have, or assume they have, authority over their state and people. As noted in the section "Plot Development: Sequences" in chapter 2, it is important to watch to see if a king's command is followed, as that will both affect the plot line and reveal how much authority that king actually has. Other authority figures in the texts include priests, elders, heads of extended families or clans, and royal messengers. Sometimes very surprising characters have authority—people like women or enemies who would not be expected in the world of that time to have status or authority. For example, in the traditions about David's rise to power, Abigail, the wife of one of the local clan chiefs, helps David avoid potentially disastrous blood vengeance against her arrogant and foolish husband, Nabal. In her persuasive and peacemaking dialogue with David, she speaks of his future, addressing him respectfully as "my lord"—words that are revealed by the later story line to be authoritative.

> When Abigail saw David, she . . . said, ". . . My lord, do not take seriously this ill-natured fellow, Nabal; for . . . folly is with him. . . . Now

then, my lord, . . . since the LORD has restrained you from bloodguilt and from taking vengeance with your own hand, . . . please forgive the trespass of your servant; for the LORD will certainly make my lord a sure house, because my lord is fighting the battles of the LORD; and evil shall not be found in you so long as you live. . . . When the LORD . . . has appointed you prince over Israel, my lord shall have no cause of grief, or pangs of conscience, for having shed blood without cause or for having saved himself." (1 Sam. 25:23–26, 28, 30–31)

One interest about David conveyed in this story is that the Lord will establish David as a prince over Israel and build him a "sure house," or dynasty. That a woman is one of the first to identify David's forthcoming importance is worth noting.

Equally surprising, a foreign ruler can sometimes be granted authority for undertaking certain actions; here the source of the authority is usually God, and the point is made that God has power even over other nations and their leaders. The political impetus for the people's return from exile is vividly described at the beginning of Ezra as happening under the authority of the king of Persia. See how the Persian king is directly "stirred up" by God so that he becomes an authority who carries out God's will, which is expressed as the reestablishment of the temple in Jerusalem:

The LORD stirred up the spirit of King Cyrus of Persia so that he . . . in a written edict declared: "Thus says King Cyrus of Persia: The LORD, the God of heaven, has given me all the kingdoms of the earth, and he has charged me to build him a house at Jerusalem in Judah. Any of those among you who are of his people—may their God be with them!—are now permitted to go up to Jerusalem in Judah, and rebuild the house of the LORD, the God of Israel." (Ezra 1:1–3)

It is helpful to see how a text makes an argument establishing the power of a particular leader and validating that leader's mandate to carry out certain actions. By looking at the highlighted phrases in the following passage we see how the overall text establishes Joshua's authority to take over as Moses's successor as the people of Israel are entering the land.

> After the death of Moses the servant of the LORD, the Lord spoke
> to Joshua son of Nun, Moses' assistant, saying, "My servant Moses
> is dead. Now proceed to cross the Jordan, you and all this people,
> into the land. . . . No one shall be able to stand against you all the
> days of your life. As I was with Moses, so I will be with you; I will not
> fail you or forsake you. Be strong and courageous; for you shall put
> this people in possession of the land that I swore to their ancestors
> to give them. Only be strong and very courageous, being careful to
> act in accordance with all the law that my servant Moses commanded
> you . . . so that you may be successful wherever you go. . . . I hereby
> command you: Be strong and courageous; do not be frightened or
> dismayed, for the Lord your God is with you wherever you go." . . .
> [The people] answered Joshua: "All that you have commanded us we
> will do, and wherever you send us we will go. Just as we obeyed Moses
> in all things, so we will obey you. Only may the Lord your God be with
> you, as he was with Moses!" (Josh. 1:1–2, 5–7, 9, 16–17)

Elements of the authority argument marshaled here for Joshua include that the Lord speaks directly to him, Moses's memory and
authority are mentioned frequently, and Joshua is given both a direct command to lead the people and the promise that God will be
with him as with Moses. These words from God are then further
reinforced by the words of the people, who recognize Joshua's authority when they in one voice agree to follow and obey Joshua just
as they followed Moses.

Other voices in a text besides that of God can also work to reinforce the authority of a character. Often the narrator or storyteller
will line up the phrases that argue for a person's mandate, or sometimes a character who also has authority, like a king, will grant that
power to another. Both of these strategies are used in the postexilic
story about Ezra, who was appointed by the Persian king to establish
the administration of the law of God in Judah and to carry financial
offerings in order to reestablish the services and offerings of worship
in the temple in Jerusalem.

> Ezra son of Seraiah, . . . son of the chief priest Aaron—this Ezra went
> up from Babylonia. He was a scribe skilled in the law of Moses that

the LORD the God of Israel had given; and the king granted him all
that he asked, for the hand of the Lord his God was upon him. . . .
       This is a copy of the letter that King Artaxerxes gave . . . : "Arta-
xerxes, king of kings, to the priest Ezra, the scribe of the law of
the God of heaven. . . . For you are sent by the king and his seven
counselors . . . to convey the silver and gold that the king and his
counselors have freely offered to the God of Israel, whose dwelling is
in Jerusalem. . . . And you, Ezra, according to the God-given wisdom
you possess, appoint magistrates and judges who may judge all the
people . . . who know the laws of your God; and you shall teach those
who do not know them." (Ezra 7:1, 5–6, 11–12, 14–15, 25)

The phrases in verses 1–6 are in the authority of the storyteller. These
phrases establish Ezra's influential priestly lineage (excerpted here
for brevity) all the way back to Aaron, Moses's brother, and give
direct descriptions of Ezra's skill and closeness to God. Verses 11–25
reinforce Ezra's authority by his mandate from the king, the king's
own words to Ezra, royal recognition of Ezra's wisdom, mention
of donations from the royal treasury, and a three-part command
to Ezra about what he is being appointed to do. As evidenced by
the highlighted phrases, the text has made a convincing case that
Ezra is truly the one who has been appointed to carry out both the
Lord's and the king's will in Judah and Jerusalem. The text has also
supported the value of the reestablishment of the temple and the
law in the restored community in Jerusalem and the leadership of
a priest and scribe like Ezra.

Crafting Repetition

When a speaker really wants to get a point across to an audience,
it is useful to repeat the thought so everyone has a clear sense of
the idea. In other words, repetition can drive a point home to an
audience. Those two sentences are in fact an example of repetition
at work—the sentences did not use verbatim repetition, but the
words and ideas are similar enough that virtually the same idea is
expressed. Can you remember instances where your parents or some

Questions
for Careful Readers

How is repetition used to craft a persuasive argument or make a point or idea more evident and forceful in the text?

Where do you see repetition working across adjacent texts, and where does it work across lengthy spans of chapters?

other authority figures went on and on about something they wanted you to do until you did what they wanted in order to end all their nagging? If so, you have experienced the power of repetition.

Here is a vivid example of repetition at work in biblical historical writing, in a passage where the prophet Samuel describes what he has heard from God about how a king will act. Not only is there repetition of the phrase "he will take" (highlighted below) but also variations of pronouns referring to the king are repeated (boldface).

> He said, "These will be the ways of the king who will reign over you: he will take your sons and appoint them to his chariots and to be his horsemen, and to run before his chariots; and he will appoint for himself commanders of thousands and commanders of fifties, and some to plow his ground and to reap his harvest, and to make his implements of war and the equipment of his chariots. He will take your daughters to be perfumers and cooks and bakers. He will take the best of your fields and vineyards and olive orchards and give them to his courtiers. He will take one-tenth of your grain and of your vineyards and give it to his officers and his courtiers. He will take your male and female slaves, and the best of your cattle and donkeys, and put them to his work. He will take one-tenth of your flocks, and you shall be his slaves. And in that day you will cry out because of your king, whom you have chosen for yourselves; but the LORD will not answer you in that day." (1 Sam. 8:11–18)

Notice that this text builds on the authoritative role of prophets to convey very powerful words from God about human behavior and ethical standards. This passage occurs in a section of 1 Samuel that relates traditions about the time when early Israel was moving from clan social organization toward kingship, a process that raised strong and varied memories about the costs and benefits of monarchy. This passage warns about the costs of kingship. By repeating that the king

The Dramatic Use of Repetition

While repetition can be tedious, sometimes repetition can be used dramatically to impact and persuade an audience. Consider the conclusion of Dr. Martin Luther King Jr.'s speech of August 28, 1963, at the Lincoln Memorial in Washington, DC.

> And so even though we face the difficulties of today and tomorrow, I still have a dream. It is a dream deeply rooted in the American dream.
>
> I have a dream that one day this nation will rise up and live out the true meaning of its creed: "We hold these truths to be self-evident, that all men are created equal."
>
> I have a dream that one day on the red hills of Georgia, the sons of former slaves and the sons of former slave owners will be able to sit down together at the table of brotherhood.
>
> I have a dream that one day even the state of Mississippi, a state sweltering with the heat of injustice, sweltering with the heat of oppression, will be transformed into an oasis of freedom and justice.
>
> I have a dream that my four little children will one day live in a nation where they will not be judged by the color of their skin but by the content of their character.
>
> I have a dream today![a]

a. Martin Luther King Jr., "I Have a Dream," *American Rhetoric*, accessed December 30, 2012, http://www.americanrhetoric.com/speeches/mlkihaveadream.htm.

will take the family members, goods, and land of the peasant farmers and put all that to his own advantage, the impression of a king's ruthlessness, selfishness, and greed is created. Noticing repetition is one of the most efficient ways a reader can come to understand what the text is trying to convey.

Setting Up Analogies between Accounts

Repetition of words and phrases not only works within a small section of text but also can work across texts that are separated by many chapters. We will see a version of this below in the section about establishing patterns across large portions of text. Here, we want to see how repetition between two passages creates a link

Question for Careful Readers

What analogies are created between accounts, in which two figures or events are shaped so that they resonate with each other and thus inform the reader about the characteristics of both ends of the analogy?

between them. In addition to the repetition of phrases, this link is an analogy between two stories, in which the story line in one passage closely resembles the situation in the other so that a comparison is set up.

Compare the following two passages:

After the death of Moses . . . , the LORD spoke to Joshua . . . , saying, "My servant Moses is dead. Now proceed to cross the Jordan, you and all this people, into the land that I am giving to them. . . . Be strong and courageous; for you shall put this people in possession of the land that I swore to their ancestors to give them. Only be strong and very courageous, being careful to act in accordance with all the law that my servant Moses commanded you; do not turn from it to the right hand or to the left, so that you may be successful wherever you go. This book of the law shall not depart out of your mouth; you shall meditate on it day and night, so that you may be careful to act in accordance with all that is written in it. For then you shall make your way prosperous, and then you shall be successful. I hereby command you: Be strong and courageous; do not be frightened or dismayed, for the LORD your God is with you wherever you go." (Josh. 1:1–2, 6–9)

When David's time to die drew near, he charged his son Solomon, saying: ". . . Be strong, be courageous, and keep the charge of the LORD your God, walking in his ways and keeping his statutes, his commandments, his ordinances, and his testimonies, as it is written in the law of Moses, so that you may prosper in all that you do and wherever you turn. Then the LORD will establish his word that he spoke concerning me: 'If your heirs take heed to their way, to walk before me in faithfulness with all their heart and with all their soul, there shall not fail you a successor on the throne of Israel.'" (1 Kings 2:1–4)

The text is highlighted in different ways to illustrate the repetition of exact or similar phrases between these two texts. Both texts occur in their story context as a transition between a dying leader and a successor—the first is the Lord's words to Joshua, Moses's successor, and the second is David's words to Solomon, his heir. The speeches are separated by perhaps two hundred years of history in the biblical chronology. The first thing to notice is how this technique builds on the authority argument we noted above. Joshua has already been established by God's word as a leader; thus he is an appropriate parallel for what David wants to say to his heir. Then, you can see clearly that similar words are said to the new leader in each case, reflecting the values and ideals of the religious heritage underlying the stories in the Deuteronomistic History, from which both texts come. These values include faithfulness to God and being careful to follow in all God's ways as they are found in the law given to Moses. When two speeches in a similar situation are so parallel, more than one effect occurs: not only are the values reflected in the text reinforced by the repetition but also a resonance is set up between the texts. You might imagine that the highlighted words in each passage are like a link between websites—click on one, and the other passage opens up. The historical writing in the biblical books uses repetition across stories in this way to draw attention to interests and values that span the ages and traditions.

Using Direct Evaluation

Some ways that texts express views and opinions are quite obvious, while other shaping is more subtle. One of the most obvious methods by which texts communicate their points of view is that of direct evaluation. This is a familiar human interaction. Staff in an organization or business experience direct evaluation if they undergo a performance review. Every student is familiar with direct evaluation when he or she gets an assignment back from a professor—for better or worse!

Questions for Careful Readers

What direct evaluation is included in the text?

How is it expressed, and what values, judgments, and ideals does it convey?

Consider the following text that contains direct evaluation:

> Then the Israelites did what was evil in the sight of the Lord and worshiped the Baals; and they abandoned the Lord, the God of their ancestors, who had brought them out of the land of Egypt; they followed other gods, from among the gods of the peoples who were all around them, and bowed down to them; and they provoked the Lord to anger. They abandoned the LORD, and worshiped Baal and the Astartes. (Judg. 2:11–13)

Even if you did not know that the "Baals" and "Astartes" were ancient divine figures or what the text means when it refers to God "who had brought them out of the land of Egypt," it is unmistakable that this passage does not approve of certain behaviors. The phrases highlighted convey this negative evaluation quite clearly. In this case, it is a definitively negative evaluation, so this technique is being used here as a way of dissociation—these actions are *not* recommended by this text!

This type of transparent expression of evaluation is found in various texts of the historical books. In the Deuteronomistic History, these same phrases are used numerous times to impart the values of the text. In particular the phrase "to do evil/good in the sight of the LORD" is used over sixty-five times in the book of Deuteronomy and the Deuteronomistic History. (This phrase is also used in 2 Chronicles in passages that are parallel to and probably dependent on passages in Kings.) Both the direct strong language of evaluation and the repetition have the effect of making the attitude of the text crystal clear to the audience.

Now consider this excerpt from 2 Kings 17 that evaluates the conquest of the northern state of Israel by the Assyrian Empire, an event that occurred in 722 BCE.

> In the ninth year of Hoshea the king of Assyria captured Samaria; he carried the Israelites away to Assyria. . . . This occurred because the people of Israel had sinned against the Lord their God. . . . They had worshiped other gods. . . . They set up for themselves pillars and sacred poles on every high hill . . . ; there they made offerings on all

the high places. . . . They did wicked things, provoking the Lord to anger. . . . They despised his statutes, and his covenant that he made with their ancestors, . . . and they sold themselves to do evil in the sight of the Lord, provoking him to anger. Therefore the Lord was very angry with Israel and removed them out of his sight. (2 Kings 17:6–7, 10–11, 15, 17–18)

And consider this excerpt from 1 Chronicles about Saul, the king of the northern tribes of Israel just before David, after he was killed in battle against the Philistines:

So Saul died for his unfaithfulness; he was unfaithful to the Lord in that he did not keep the command of the LORD; moreover, he had consulted a medium, seeking guidance, and did not seek guidance from the LORD. Therefore the LORD put him to death and turned the kingdom over to David son of Jesse. (1 Chron. 10:13–14)

In these passages the highlighted phrases convey the clear and relentless judgments of the texts. The 2 Kings text clearly wants to let its audience hear that Israel (the northern state) was conquered because God was so angry about the sinful actions of the people that destruction and removal of the state was justified. Note how the text uses phrases like those we saw in Judges 2—this is an example of repetition across large sections of the biblical books. Note also how the piling up of negative direct evaluation is interspersed with "reasons" for God's response, in particular, the people's religious behaviors that the author clearly found sinful, like worshiping other gods. These are detailed and accumulated to show that the people had abandoned the God who had been gracious to them. The 1 Chronicles text casts an extremely negative judgment on Saul, again giving reasons for the direct evaluation. These passages, which we might call reflections or "sermons" on events related in the stories, show the capacity of the text to be explicit in its evaluation of certain behaviors and events. In the next chapter, on examining history in the text, we will look at how the role of God in historical events is portrayed in biblical books. For now, the point is to see how phrases and evaluative judgments give the audience a clear picture of the interests the texts are endorsing.

Creating Patterns

The techniques of direct evaluation and repetition are often combined by texts to establish a pattern across larger sections of a document or biblical books. You will notice this method of communicating values when you see phrases used over and over again as you read. Patterns are often created across large sections of texts, sometimes even spanning several books.

Look at the following texts:

Questions for Careful Readers

What patterns are set up in the text and, in particular, across texts? What are the elements of the pattern in each case?

How do direct evaluation and pattern setting work together to convey judgments across stories?

What does the omission of an established pattern communicate about a figure, event, or idea?

Now Rehoboam son of Solomon reigned in Judah. . . . Judah did what was evil in the sight of the Lord; they provoked him to jealousy with their sins that they committed, more than all that their ancestors had done. (1 Kings 14:21–22)

Nadab son of Jeroboam began to reign over Israel in the second year of King Asa of Judah; he reigned over Israel two years. He did what was evil in the sight of the Lord, walking in the way of his ancestor and in the sin that he caused Israel to commit. (1 Kings 15:25–26)

In the thirty-first year of King Asa of Judah, Omri began to reign over Israel. . . . Omri did what was evil in the sight of the Lord; he did more evil than all who were before him. (1 Kings 16:23, 25)

In the third year of King Hoshea son of Elah of Israel, Hezekiah son of King Ahaz of Judah began to reign. . . . He did what was right in the sight of the Lord just as his ancestor David had done. (2 Kings 18:1, 3)

This series of texts gives just a few of the thirty-three formulas in the Deuteronomistic History that introduce the reigns of kings (called "regnal formulas") using set phrases. These formulas function to create a value judgment about the kings (in addition to giving other information about things like the length of reign). The pattern of introducing each king using a form that almost always includes the evaluative phrase about doing good or evil sets up the expectation in the audience that the text will stand in judgment on the kings. Because you have already seen the impact of the direct evaluation, you know the types of both good and bad royal actions that would invite the evaluation: fidelity and true worship of God for a positive evaluation and sinful religious practices for a negative one. In addition to the evaluative phrase, more or fewer details are included about each king to expand the formula and justify the evaluation. Then, as the passage for each king unfolds, incidents in the form of shorter or longer stories and summary information are included for each king's reign. Because the audience's expectations have already been set up by the evaluative formula, the stories and summaries selected for each king are influenced by the shaping of the evaluation.

Setting Up Models

The next technique we will study to see how an ancient text makes its interests known is called "modeling." This technique uses the concepts of presence, association, and repetition to help persuade a reader or hearer about certain points. In a sense, modeling is a version of setting up a pattern, but here focused on one particular character. Modeling works in a text by setting up a particular character from one part of the story as a model with which other characters can be compared. Invoking a model to support an idea works as long as the figure is already known to the audience, so the model usually is a famous or outstanding figure in some way, either impressively good, strong, or righteous, or, in the case of a dissociation, intensely bad. The model acts as a kind of authority or ideal figure against which other figures or ideas can be tested.

In our modern context, the frequent references we hear in the media to the "Founding Fathers" of the United States are examples of modeling. In these references, a writer of a blog, website, article, or editorial invokes the memory or words of one or more of the Founding Fathers in order to support a point. Because George Washington, Thomas Jefferson, Benjamin Franklin, and others are so well known as Revolutionary War heroes and early United States statesmen, using their names lends weight to a point in a modern text or speech. However, a search of the internet will show that the modern political positions for which an invocation of the Founding Fathers can be used are quite varied—the reference is used by a wide variety of authors for differing purposes. We will see the same phenomenon in the ancient historical texts.

Questions for Careful Readers

What figures are set up as models for other characters in the historical books?

What values and ideas does the model express, and how do those values and ideas transfer to the other figures who follow the model?

As we noted above in the section about presence, David's name appears many times outside the stories where he is the main character, almost always to add insight or value judgment to the passages that cite him. The purposes of David as a model, however, vary among the biblical books. We will examine two groups of books, the Deuteronomistic History and Chronicles-Ezra-Nehemiah, beginning with these passages from the Deuteronomistic History.

From an evaluation of King Solomon:

> For when Solomon was old, his wives turned away his heart after other gods; and his heart was not true to the LORD his God, as was the heart of his father David. . . . So Solomon did what was evil in the sight of the LORD, and did not completely follow the LORD, as his father David had done. (1 Kings 11:4, 6)

From a prophecy addressed to King Jeroboam, first king of Israel:

> Yet you have not been like my servant David, who kept my commandments and followed me with all his heart, doing only that which was

right in my sight, but you have done evil above all those who were before you and have gone and made for yourself other gods, . . . provoking me to anger. (1 Kings 14:8–9)

From the regnal evaluation of King Abijam of Judah:

His heart was not true to the LORD his God, like the heart of his father David. . . . David did what was right in the sight of the LORD, and did not turn aside from anything that he commanded him. (1 Kings 15:3, 5)

From the regnal evaluation of King Hezekiah of Judah:

He did what was right in the sight of the LORD just as his ancestor David had done. He removed the high places, broke down the pillars, and cut down the sacred pole. (2 Kings 18:3–4)

Passages like these show us how David as a model is used to rate the behaviors of later kings in the stories of the Deuteronomistic History. Particularly in regnal formulas throughout 1 and 2 Kings, but also in summaries and speeches, David is named in order to compare other kings to the exceptional qualities the text attributes to him. The values with which David is associated are being faithful to the Lord (using the phrase "his heart was true to the LORD"), doing what was right in the sight of the Lord, and keeping the commandments of God. Where details are given in these regnal formulas and in the phrases that expand the formulas, particular behaviors that David enacted generally have to do with exclusive loyalty to and worship of God, in that he avoided turning to other gods or using religious objects associated with the worship of other gods, such as the high places (local sanctuaries) or pillars or sacred poles (cult objects). When later kings are rated as being like David, they generally receive a positive evaluation, but when they engaged in practices that did not live up to David's standards, the text rates them negatively.

How is David as a model used in the historical books of the later Second Temple period? When we examine references to David in Chronicles, Ezra, and Nehemiah, all written hundreds of years after David's time, he is still used as a model. However, the values associated with him are somewhat changed from those of the Deuteronomistic History. Consider the passages below.

From King Solomon's prayer at the dedication of the temple:

> Therefore, O LORD, God of Israel, keep for your servant, my father David, that which you promised him, saying, "There shall never fail you a successor before me to sit on the throne of Israel, if only your children keep to their way, to walk in my law as you have walked before me." (2 Chron. 6:16)

From the regnal evaluation of King Ahaz of Judah:

> Ahaz was twenty years old when he began to reign. . . . He did not do what was right in the sight of the LORD, as his ancestor David had done, but he . . . made cast images for the Baals. (2 Chron. 28:1–2)

Because Chronicles probably used 2 Kings as a source, when it includes regnal formulas from 2 Kings it reflects a similar valuation of David as a model. Later kings are rated on how well they follow in the law of the Lord, whether they do what is right in the sight of the Lord, and whether they keep their worship free of condemned worship practices.

However, these later historical books also emphasize another aspect when they use David's memory to communicate values and ideas. Look at the passages below.

From the reign of Josiah, one of the last kings of Judah, arranging the Passover festival:

> [Josiah] said to the Levites . . . , "Make preparations by your ancestral houses by your divisions, following the written directions of King David of Israel." (2 Chron. 35:3–4)

From the story of the rebuilding of the temple after the exile:

> When the builders laid the foundation of the temple of the LORD,
> the priests . . . were stationed to praise the LORD with trumpets, and
> the Levites . . . with cymbals, according to the directions of King
> David of Israel. (Ezra 3:10)

From "Nehemiah's Memoir" about the dedication of the rebuilt city
wall after the exile, arranging a celebration procession to include
the following:

> Some of the young priests with trumpets: Zechariah . . . and his
> kindred, . . . with the musical instruments of David the man of God.
> (Neh. 12:35–36)

These passages reveal an interest in the religious ceremony and
rituals of the temple in Jerusalem when it was rebuilt after the exile.
The texts of Chronicles, Ezra, and Nehemiah associate the origins
of these religious institutions with David. David is being remembered in the traditions of Judah as the founder of the temple and
its religious ceremonies, as well as its religious officials, like priests
(Levites were a branch of the priesthood), and its musical offerings.
When these texts invoke David's memory, they are grounding the
postexilic religious observances in their time of origin under David,
thus lending the observances stature and importance in the time of
the writers. Here we see the technique of modeling used to convey
particular aspects of David as a model, an aspect that the texts of
the Deuteronomistic History did not choose to emphasize.

The combination of direct evaluation and setting up patterns
can also work to dissociate an audience's sympathies from certain
ideas, and the biblical story uses this strategy as well. The Deuteronomistic History rates the kings of the northern state, Israel, as
uniformly lacking in loyalty to the Lord or faithful worship. The
bad news starts with Jeroboam, the king who has rebelled against
David's dynasty, who is aware that he must turn the religious and
political loyalty of his people away from Judah.

> So the king . . . made two calves of gold. He said to the people,
> "You have gone up to Jerusalem long enough. Here are your gods,

> O Israel, who brought you up out of the land of Egypt." . . . This
> matter became sin to the house of Jeroboam, so as to cut it off and
> to destroy it from the face of the earth. (1 Kings 12:28; 13:34)

The direct language of sin and destruction clearly communicates the
text's negative judgment about Jeroboam's actions. He then becomes
the standard by which all other Israelite kings are judged, and all of
them come up short on loyalty, true worship, and allegiance to the
Lord. Note how a subsequent wicked northern dynasty is rated by
Jeroboam's standard but manages to be even worse:

> Omri did what was evil in the sight of the LORD; he did more evil
> than all who were before him. For he walked in all the way of Jero-
> boam . . . , and in the sins that he caused Israel to commit, provok-
> ing the LORD, the God of Israel, to anger by their idols. . . . Ahab
> son of Omri began to reign over Israel. . . . And as if it had been a
> light thing for him to walk in the sins of Jeroboam . . . , [he] went
> and served Baal, and worshiped him. . . . Ahab also made a sacred
> pole. Ahab did more to provoke the anger of the LORD, the God of
> Israel, than had all the kings of Israel who were before him. (1 Kings
> 16:25–26, 29, 31, 33)

The text's insistence on the religious standards by which disloyalty
to the Lord is judged is clear here, and the kings of the north match
or exceed the negative model of the founder of the state, Jeroboam.

Creating a negative model is not the only way that a pattern can
be used in a text to communicate dissociation or to discourage an
audience's interest in or adherence to an idea. On occasion, the
omission of a pattern that has already been established can convey
a disapproving evaluation by the text. For example, the books of
1 and 2 Chronicles tell largely the same story as the Deuteronomistic
History about the time of the monarchy between about 1000 and
600 BCE. This is evident in the amount of material shared between
1 and 2 Kings and 1 and 2 Chronicles, including in many instances
parallel stories complete with evaluative regnal formulas about the
kings of Judah. However, even though Chronicles evidently knew the
traditions about the northern state, Israel, these books almost always

completely omit stories about Israel. Where events related in the text overlap with figures of events in Israel—a military event or intermarriage, for example—the northern information is related simply to make the story about Judah complete. The pattern of kings' reigns and regnal evaluations from the Deuteronomistic History is broken, an omission that clearly communicates that Chronicles has no interest in the political fortunes of Israel as a state, because it lacked legitimacy in comparison with Judah and the Davidic monarchy.

Creating Dramatic Impact

Another technique that historical books use to convey their interests is a part of their storytelling artistry that also functions to emphasize certain ideas the text communicates. This is the practice of using drama and intensity to focus an audience's attention. Anyone who has seen an action movie will know how this works—the scenes that have everyone on the edge of their seats are the ones where cars go careening around corners at high speed, things blow up, and the aliens or vampires descend on their helpless victims. In the historical books of the Old Testament, action does not get quite as explosive and visual as in a movie, but scenes that rate as dramatic in an ancient context have a similar impact. Usually the point is not in the drama itself but in the values conveyed around the dramatic events.

An example from 2 Kings will illustrate.

> **Questions for Careful Readers**
>
> How does the story create dramatic impact through strong words, dramatic language, vivid scenes, and powerful characters?
>
> What does the dramatic impact tell you about where the story focuses its interests?

Now when Athaliah, [King] Ahaziah's mother, saw that her son was dead, she set about to destroy all the royal family. But Jehosheba, . . . Ahaziah's sister, took Joash son of Ahaziah, and stole him away from among the king's children who were about to be killed; she put him and his nurse in a bedroom. Thus she hid him from Athaliah, so that he was not killed. (2 Kings 11:1–2)

The murder of an entire royal family by a powerful queen mother is the stuff of violent court intrigues, worthy of any high-fantasy novel or television miniseries. The regnal formula of Athaliah's husband when he became king of Judah already warned the audience about Athaliah, because she was related to the notorious dynasty of Omri and Ahab in Israel (2 Kings 8:18). As we saw above in the section on the use of models, the text has already worked to show the audience that Israel in the north had only evil kings who did not follow the ways of the Lord. And when Athaliah seizes the throne by violence, she seems to fulfill the text's highly negative expectations of her.

However, the drama is not over in the story; seven years later, the boy king who has been hidden away is supported by loyal priests and military offices to regain his rightful throne in a countercoup. After the loyalists set the stage for the action of crowning the new king in the temple, the story reaches its climax.

> When Athaliah heard the noise of the guard and of the people, she went into the house of the LORD . . . ; when she looked, there was the king standing by the pillar. . . . Athaliah tore her clothes and cried, "Treason! Treason!" Then the priest Jehoiada commanded the captains who were set over the army, "Bring her out. . . ." So they laid hands on her; . . . and there she was put to death. (2 Kings 11:13–16)

The evil queen mother has met her match and her end. In the context of the regnal evaluations we noted above, the drama of the story reinforces the warning against the sinful ways associated with those who are not loyal to the Lord and to the dynasty of David.

This technique of creating drama to focus an audience's attention can also be illustrated from a story in the book of Ezra. This scene from Ezra takes place in the postexilic period when the descendants of those who had been exiled to Babylon were restoring the life and institutions of Judah under the auspices of the Persian Empire. As we saw above, the book introduces Ezra as a scribe and priest who was appointed by the Persian king to restore the temple and to reestablish the law and courts of the people in Judah. This text reports that one of the problems Ezra confronted was that the people of Jerusalem had intermarried with neighboring peoples in contradiction to the law, which set a strict marriage boundary in order to protect the purity and worship life of the people. Ezra reacts in this way:

> When I heard this, I tore my garment and my mantle, and pulled hair from my head and beard, and . . . I sat appalled until the evening sacrifice. At the evening sacrifice I . . . fell on my knees, spread out my hands to the Lord my God, and said, "O my God, I am too ashamed and embarrassed to lift my face to you, my God, for our iniquities have risen higher than our heads, and our guilt has mounted up to the heavens. . . ." While Ezra prayed and made confession, weeping and throwing himself down . . . the people also wept bitterly. (Ezra 9:3–6; 10:1)

The highlighted phrases in this passage convey details in a way that dramatically sets the scene and expresses the emotional tone of Ezra's reaction. The language of embarrassment, tearing garments, pulling out hair, and bitter weeping reflects ancient cultural practices of deep grief and shame that the ancient audience would have immediately recognized. The technique to notice in this passage is the use of drama and loaded language to construct a scene that conveys the importance of these events. This is not neutral reporting of a mild, inconsequential event, like a Facebook post about what you are planning to do this weekend. Rather, the dramatic emotional and religious impact of this text suggests that this issue of social boundaries goes to the heart of the community's survival and purity.

Using Detail to Increase Presence

The final technique we will examine among the ways that a text expresses its interests is that of adding details that serve to focus on particular aspects of the story and to increase the presence of those aspects for the audience. Often the detail is not strictly needed for the audience to follow the story but serves other purposes. Sometimes an extensive amount of information is added, other times a smaller amount. However, when a text slows down to spend time on specifics, you can assume that these are an important part of what the text wants to convey. You know the power of details through any study that relies on meticulous description to convey information—a biology textbook, for example. Or imagine how quickly a fashion writer would be fired for sending a report from the Paris runway show that simply read, "She wore a blue dress," and missed the exquisite details that made *that* dress wonderful. In a parallel manner, the strategy of creating presence through extended attention and focus is used in all the historical books.

Questions for Careful Readers

What details are included in the text?

Where does the flow of the story in the text slow down to include extra attention to particulars, including formats like lists and extended description?

We can see the use of details at work in a simple story from the legends about the prophet Elijah. This particular story is set in northern Israel during a time when a severe drought was ravaging the land, making it difficult to survive, especially for the peasants. Elijah is sent by God to a widow and told that the widow will feed him. It is worth quoting the story in its entirety so you can see how it works.

As [the widow] was going to bring [Elijah some water], he called to her and said, "Bring me a morsel of bread in your hand." But she said, "As the Lord your God lives, I have nothing baked, only a handful of meal in a jar, and a little oil in a jug; I am now gathering a couple of sticks, so that I may go home and prepare it for myself and my son, that we may eat it, and die." Elijah said to her, "Do not be afraid; go and do as you have said; but first make me a little cake of it and bring it to me, and afterwards make something for yourself and your son. For thus says the Lord the God of Israel: The jar of meal will not be emptied and the jug of oil will not fail until the day that the Lord sends rain on the earth." She went and did as Elijah said, so that she as well as he and her household ate for many days. The jar of meal was not emptied, neither did the jug of oil fail, according to the word of the Lord that he spoke by Elijah. (1 Kings 17:11–16)

Even though this story is short, there are details included. You can see the impact of details if you consider the following. The story would have made sense if it had said, "Elijah asked the widow for some food, but she had very little available. Elijah told her to prepare some anyway because God would provide, so she did and there was plenty for both her family and Elijah." That is very brief and not very interesting, even though it makes the same point as this story. In contrast, the text includes particulars about the handful of meal in the jar, the little oil in a jug, the widow gathering sticks, the sorrowful detail that this will be the last meal for the widow and her son, and how Elijah asks her to make a little cake for him, and then it repeats the jar and jug details three times. These details, while not strictly needed, add to the interests that the story conveys—the impact of the drought on the poor and vulnerable, the compassion of God through the work of Elijah, the provision of God for the poor, and the power of God to bring well-being even to those who do not matter much in the society of that time. These interests would be minimized or lost without the details, so the details themselves help convey what the story means.

Sometimes much more detail is included in a text, and in formats that are less user friendly for a storyteller's art. These formats include lists, which simply enumerate names or items (like a genealogical list of names), and meticulous and lengthy descriptions of objects (like a report of all the utensils for the temple). When a long list or extensive description is inserted into a narrative, it will be part of the story and convey particular points while also interrupting the narrative flow. We may be tempted not to pay attention to such lists or descriptions because they seem tedious. However, it is worth realizing that these formats function deliberately as part of the text even if they are fairly awkward in the flow of the story. As we noted above, lengthy reports help make points or ideas *present* to an audience. However, lists and lengthy descriptions produce other effects, and we can see more about the point of view of a text when we consider that. It is worth reflecting on what these formats communicate, even if we are not interested in the details themselves.

Words That Change History

Memorable speeches and books contain not only well-crafted words but also words that are capable of changing decisions and events of their time. Below are some examples.

"The Gettysburg Address," Abraham Lincoln, November 19, 1863

From these honored dead we take increased devotion to that cause for which they gave the last full measure of devotion—that we here highly resolve that these dead shall not have died in vain, that this nation under God shall have a new birth of freedom, and that government of the people, by the people, for the people shall not perish from the earth.[a]

"First Inaugural Speech," Franklin Delano Roosevelt, March 4, 1933

The only thing we have to fear is fear itself—nameless, unreasoning, unjustified terror which paralyzes needed efforts to convert retreat into advance. In every dark hour of our national life, a leadership of frankness and of vigor has met with that understanding and support of the people themselves which is essential to victory.[b]

Silent Spring, Rachel Carson, 1962

The most alarming of all man's assaults upon the environment is the contamination of the air, earth, rivers, and sea with dangerous and even lethal chemicals. This pollution is for the most part irrecoverable; the chain of evil it initiates not only in the world that must support life but in living tissues is for the most part irreversible.[c]

a. Abraham Lincoln, "The Gettysburg Address," *American Rhetoric*, accessed December 30, 2012, http://www.americanrhetoric.com/speeches/gettysburgaddress.htm.
b. Franklin Delano Roosevelt, "First Inaugural Address," *American Rhetoric*, accessed December 30, 2012, http://www.americanrhetoric.com/speeches/fdrfirstinaugural.html.
c. Rachel Carson, *Silent Spring* (New York: Houghton Mifflin, 1962), 6.

Consider this text from Ezra—here we will give only some excerpts because the list is actually sixty-two verses long (you might want to read the whole thing in the book of Ezra).

Now these were the people of the province who came from those captive exiles whom King Nebuchadnezzar of Babylon had carried captive to Babylonia; they returned to Jerusalem and Judah. . . . The descendants of Parosh, two thousand one hundred seventy-two. . . . The priests: the descendants of Jedaiah, of the house of Jeshua, nine hundred seventy-three. . . . The Levites: the descendants of Jeshua . . . , seventy-four. The singers: the descendants of Asaph, one hundred twenty-eight. . . . The following were those who came up from Tel-melah, . . . though they could not prove their families or their descent, whether they belonged to Israel. . . . [Some of the descendants of the priests] looked for their entries in the genealogical records, but they were not found there, and so they were excluded from the priesthood as unclean. (Ezra 2:1, 3, 36, 40–41, 59, 62)

Everywhere in this excerpt that you see a gap, the text has long lists of names—the type of stuff that people famously quote as bed-time reading from the Old Testament because it is sure to put you to sleep! Yet the ancient text found the lists not only important but crucial to conveying its meaning. If you think about what a class list does, or a shopping list, or a list of vocabulary that a student has to memorize, you may begin to see what these ancient lists do. Lists are used to create order or to control large amounts of information in a simple-to-use format. Lists can reflect an ordering or hierarchy for different status levels in a society or organization, detailing people or subgroups and their tasks. Lists establish a sense of complete-ness, so that a certain topic seems finished or closed. Some lists, like genealogies, make social connections among individuals and families clear, tracing the lines of descent and relationship. In certain cases, a family list or societal list can be used, either implicitly or explicitly, to communicate who is "in" and who is "out" of the group.

The Ezra text above functions in several of the ways just identi-fied, which thus reveals some of the interests of the text. First, the lists of the families who first returned from exile create the sense that these families are the "founding fathers" for later social groups in the postexilic period. If later people or families could trace their lineage back to this group, they had a more sure status in the com-munity. Some groups in the postexilic community in fact considered those who could not trace their lineage back to one of the returned exiles to be outsiders. This is reflected in the above text in the groups who could not prove that they "belonged to Israel" (Ezra 2:59). Further, the Ezra list is quite transparent about its religious function of distinguishing which priests are legitimate—only those who can trace their ancestry in the genealogical records are considered "clean," or pure, and genuine enough to serve in the reestablished religious hierarchy.

The books of Chronicles use lists and lengthy details extensively—genealogies, lists of settlements, warriors in the army, types of musicians for the temple, military divisions ordered to provide monthly service for the king, and others. First Chronicles contains an initial eight chapters of genealogical lists. It is interesting to note that these detailed genealogical lists in Chronicles include the lineages of the tribes of the northern kingdom of Israel, a state that ceased to exist when conquered by the Assyrian Empire in 722 BCE. This indicates an interest of the text in creating a portrait of "all Israel" through the use of detail as a technique. Of the other twenty-one chapters in the book, eight chapters also contain lists. Chronicles also uses extensive descriptions. Take a look at this text, which comes from the point in 1 Chronicles when David is making plans for the building of the temple, which his son Solomon will accomplish.

> Then David gave his son Solomon the plan of the vestibule of the temple, and of its houses, its treasuries, its upper rooms, and its inner chambers, and of the room for the mercy seat; and the plan of all that he had in mind: for the courts of the house of the LORD, all the surrounding chambers, the treasuries of the house of God, and the treasuries for dedicated gifts; for the divisions of the priests and of the Levites, and all the work of the service in the house of the LORD; for all the vessels for the service in the house of the LORD, the weight of gold for all golden vessels for each service, the weight of silver vessels for each service, the weight of the golden lampstands and their lamps. (1 Chron. 29:11–15)

The text goes on for several more verses of meticulous detail about what should be in the new temple. You can see the type of detail that is reported—right down to how much a gold lampstand should weigh. This text is in addition to several other lists and descriptions about the temple, its priests, Levites, and officials, and its utensils and furniture that are all associated with the name of David in 1 Chronicles. For example, a number of the lists in 1 Chronicles give information about the families and names of the Levites, a priestly order that, according to the lists, was responsible for much of the upkeep, organization, and religious rituals of the temple. The interests at work in this use of detail in Chronicles include the idea that the temple is such a central institution for the postexilic community that it must be well established. The results of the detail also include the "founding father" effect. The detailed descriptions of the temple and extensive lists about the Levites locate the founding of the temple and the Levites in David's time and associate both with that famous king's name and authority. Here we also return to one of the ideas we first explored—the centrality of David in the historical books. These examples illustrate how lists and similar forms of detail communicate much more than just names and particulars. Lists and details fulfill numerous functions in the biblical historical books, even if you do not remember every name on the list!

Conclusion

In the previous chapter, we looked at ways the biblical historical writing uses the arts of storytelling to help create pleasing and interesting stories. In this chapter, we have examined the ways that a text makes its interests evident in how it puts forward its arguments, points, and ideas. Within the storytelling format, particular points are advanced, using persuasive techniques familiar to any speakers or writers who want to make their viewpoints known. We looked at particular examples from the biblical books to see these techniques in action, like establishing authority, using repetition, and setting up models. In doing this, we not only saw how the techniques worked but also began to discover the values, opinions, evaluations, and points of view inherent in the persuasiveness of the stories. Examples include that the Lord is the ultimate authority and that kings as authority figures are evaluated on how their abilities and actions measure up "in the sight of the LORD." However, the stories do more than convey persuasive ideas. The stories also convey information about topics like leaders, political decisions, dates, events, and foreign kings and peoples who interact with ancient Israel. These topics belong to the field of history itself, and our next two chapters turn to examine how the biblical historical books work as examples of history writing.

Suggested Reading

Brueggemann, Walter. *The Practice of Prophetic Imagination: Preaching an Emancipating Word*. Minneapolis: Fortress, 2012.

Gitay, Yehoshua. "Rhetorical Criticism." Pages 135–49 in *To Each Its Own Meaning*. Edited by Steven R. Haynes and Steven L. McKenzie. Louisville: Westminster John Knox, 1993.

Hauser, Gerard. *Introduction to Rhetorical Theory*. Prospect Heights, IL: Waveland, 1991.

Perelman, Chaim. *The Realm of Rhetoric*. Notre Dame, IN: University of Notre Dame Press, 1982.

Sternberg, Meir. *The Poetics of Biblical Narrative: Ideological Literature and the Drama of Reading*. Bloomington: Indiana University Press, 1987.

Discussion Questions

1. Try this experiment: Write a speech that will convince your friends to invest money in a start-up venture you are initiating, say, to launch a new video game website. Then identify the types of persuasive arguments you made in your speech.

2. What kinds of arguments and techniques are being used in this book to persuade you about the characteristics of history writing in the Old Testament?

3. Of the interests that this chapter identified in the historical books of the Old Testament, which ones were already familiar to you as part of the theology of the Bible? Which ones were new to your understanding of the Old Testament?

4

Examining History in the Text

I n this chapter we start a full discussion of the characteristics of the biblical history writing found in the books of the Bible we have been considering: Joshua, Judges, 1 and 2 Samuel, 1 and 2 Kings, 1 and 2 Chronicles, and Ezra and Nehemiah. In the chapters thus far, we have studied significant aspects of how texts work as ancient documents and how they come out of and reflect an ancient context. These aspects are all part of how the texts also tell about history, and we will see that the narrative format, the clear interests of the texts, and the social contexts re-emerge directly in the questions we consider in these next two chapters. The particular questions we will be examining in these two chapters are the following: How do these biblical texts work as ancient history writing? When these texts tell about the past, in what ways do they do this? What are the characteristics of how the texts write history, and how do those characteristics fit into the history writing done by other ancient cultures that surrounded ancient Israel and Judah? Together with what you have learned in the previous chapters, the answers to these questions will help you to read the biblical historical writings well.

When people refer to "history," what are they thinking about? They generally have two different ideas in mind. First, "history" can mean actual past events from a standpoint later in time—the detailed complexity of events, people and interactions, dates and chronology, geographical and environmental factors, and causes and consequences that make up what actually happened. Second, "history" can mean the retelling of the past, some format that recounts the past in oral or written form. It is this second sense of the word that we will be most concerned about. That is, this book is not attempting to write a history of ancient Israel or trying to give descriptions or make judgments about what actually happened in biblical times. You can read a variety of history books in which scholars reconstruct the events, dates, people, and places told about in the Bible, but that is not our focus. Rather, we will be examining how the texts in the biblical historical books narrate the past from within their own ancient worldview and context. We will focus thus on the characteristics of biblical "history writing."

Thinking about "History"

Writing or telling about the past has some features that hold true for all types of history writing, whether ancient or contemporary. There is no way to completely reconstruct every moment, event, word, and person of the past, so any remembrance of the past is necessarily incomplete. This also means that any communication about the past will be selective about what it includes. It is important to realize that how the selection is done will influence how the history writing is shaped, whether the writer is trying to use careful analysis or has preconceived notions or attitudes. The impact of factors like these makes necessary a distinction between ancient and contemporary history writing. For example, you may already be familiar with the different ways eyewitnesses will reconstruct an accident scene—even if they were all present at the scene, their different physical and emotional perspectives will affect how they tell what happened. A police officer is responsible for taking all of these descriptions, as well as any physical evidence, such as weather conditions and tire skid marks, into account in a careful review and analysis before writing up an accident report to try to get the best version of what "actually happened."

In general, the approach used by contemporary history writers is similar to the police officer's writing up a report about an accident. When we speak in this sense of writing history, the term "historiography" is helpful, meaning literally "history writing." Modern historiography is defined as "the writing of history based on the critical examination of sources, the selections of particulars from the authentic materials, and the synthesis of particulars into a narrative that will stand the test of critical methods."[1] Contemporary historians usually try to write an account of the past that can be examined as to whether the writer has succeeded in creating a document that

- gives a fair and balanced account,
- finds and analyzes a wide number and type of sources, and
- can be evaluated by another fair-minded observer.

We can call this a "critical" account. Even in critical historiography, however, there are interests at work. Maybe the writer is producing a history that focuses on economic issues or is writing from the standpoint of constitutional law. Even fair and balanced writers may have a pointed interest in their material, for example, a concern to focus on women's lives or to bring attention to political causes of a particular social movement. Some writers may have a stronger slant that comes through in how they shape what they write even when they use critical judgment in their research and writing. For instance, some books about US history have taken the "slant" of emphasizing the important roles of African Americans in the history of the country. In any case, other critical historians and the general public may debate at length and with some heat about any histories

---

1. *Merriam-Webster's Collegiate Dictionary*, 10th ed., s.v. "historiography" (Springfield, MA: Merriam-Webster, 1999).

that are written, but critical standards still are used to write and evaluate those histories.

Ancient History Writing

As we will see, however, ancient history writing did not use the same standards and principles used in modern history writing, and it would be unfair to use modern standards to judge ancient history writing. Biblical history writing, not surprisingly, is more like other ancient history writing than like what is found in the modern period. To see what ancient history writing was like, we will give brief excerpts of texts, such as inscriptions on buildings and statues or writing in documents like tablets. These come from countries in the ancient Near East from the general time period of the biblical story (about 1300–300 BCE), including Assyrian, Hittite, Babylonian, and Egyptian writings. "In the ancient Near East history writing included such literary categories as king's lists, chronicles, annals, royal apologies, memorial inscriptions, historical poems, narratives, etc."[2]

Our use of quotes from these sources is not intended to show any direct borrowing among the texts of these neighboring states and the writing of ancient Israel and Judah. Nor do we assume that each of these cultures had the same viewpoint about history writing—each was in fact writing from within and for their own culture, including how each culture expressed its view of its own history.[3] For example, you would expect that a text about the history of England would focus on matters important to conveying the story of that country. When we look at ancient histories, we do see similarities among examples of ancient history writing that are instructive illustrations for the type of history writing we find in the Bible.[4]

2. K. Lawson Younger Jr., "The Underpinnings," in *Israel's Past in Present Research: Essays on Ancient Israelite Historiography*, ed. V. Philips Long (Winona Lake, IN: Eisenbrauns, 1999), 327.

3. Ibid., 316.

4. For a brief review, see H. Cazelles, "Biblical and Prebiblical Historiography," in Long, *Israel's Past in Present Research*, 98–128.

Writing in the Ancient Near East

Writing was an activity developed in the ancient Near East around 3000 BCE, starting with cuneiform and hieroglyphic writing in Mesopotamia and Egypt. Hieroglyphic writing systems used pictograms to represent ideas and consonantal parts of words, and cuneiform used wedge-shaped impressions to create signs denoting syllables or consonantal parts of words.

Writing using an alphabetic system of signs that designate letters making up a word was developed by the Phoenicians and then the Canaanites in the second millennium BCE. Ancient Hebrew developed from the Canaanite alphabet.

Literacy in the ancient world was probably limited to members of the upper classes and to scribes employed by royal, administrative, and temple institutions. Writing reflected the needs of administrative officials to keep track of transactions like sales, taxes, lists, and personal or official letters. Writing also allowed the development of "literature" in the form of royal and religious public inscriptions, private documents, and religious literature.

Many people in lower classes probably had at best only functional literacy, enough to write or recognize their names and a few words for social and economic transactions. Most would have functioned in an oral world where memoirs, prayers, hymns, proverbs, and stories were memorized and handed down to the next generations. However, there were probably connections and overlaps between the oral and written cultures, one continuing to influence the other as both developed. And the public reading of official, royal, or religious documents, or visible writing on walls, buildings, and monuments, would have communicated information and values to an illiterate populace.[a]

a. For further information, see Philip J. King and Lawrence E. Stager, "Literacy and Schools," in *Life in Biblical Israel*, Library of Ancient Israel (Louisville: Westminster John Knox, 2001), 300–317; Susan Niditch, *Oral World and Written Word: Ancient Israelite Literature* (Louisville: Westminster John Knox, 1996); Christopher A. Rollston, *Writing and Literacy in the World of Ancient Israel: Epigraphic Evidence from the Iron Age* (Atlanta: Society of Biblical Literature, 2010); and David W. Jamieson-Drake, *Scribes and Schools in Monarchic Judah: A Socio-Archaeological Approach* (Sheffield: Sheffield Academic Press, 1991).

The period of time from which we will pull examples of ancient history writing covers about one thousand years. Toward the end of the period, a new understanding of history writing was beginning to emerge in one of the civilizations of the Mediterranean world, Greece. Greek writers took the first steps in developing what we understand as critical and analytical history writing. History writing among the Greeks in the fifth century BCE and after, especially Herodotus and Thucydides, shows a marked development in the way historical accounts are handled. Thucydides writes in the introduction to his *History of the Peloponnesian War*,

> We may claim instead to have used only the plainest evidence and to have reached conclusions which are reasonably accurate. . . . Either I was present myself at the events which I have described or else I heard of them from eye-witnesses whose reports I have checked with as much thoroughness as possible.[5]

Thucydides and later writers cultivated the development of a more critical attitude toward their sources than is evident in other ancient writing, including deliberate use of firsthand and eyewitness accounts and an evaluation of the reliability of their sources.[6] However, the judgment of most scholars is that even though the Greeks were forerunners in this development, these were only the first steps in the growth of what we would consider critical historiography, and that most Greek writers also continued to use many of the nonanalytical conventions and assumptions of the writing of the ancient world.[7]

In our discussion of biblical history writing in this chapter, we will focus on how biblical history constructs an account of the past

5. Thucydides, *History of the Peloponnesian War*, trans. R. Warner (Baltimore: Penguin, 1972), quoted in Peter Machinist, "The Voice of the Historian in the Ancient Near East and Mediterranean World," *Interpretation* 57 (2003): 119.

6. Lester Grabbe, *A History of the Jews and Judaism in the Second Temple Period*, vol. 1, *Yehud: A History of the Persian Province of Judah* (London: T&T Clark International, 2004), 123.

7. For discussion of the many complex issues involved, see Machinist, "Voice of the Historian," 117–37; Arnaldo Momigliano, *The Classical Foundations of Modern Historiography* (Berkeley: University of California Press, 1990), 5–53; Grabbe, *History of the Jews*, 118–23; T. P. Wiseman, "Classical History: A Sketch, with Three Artifacts," in *Understanding the History of Ancient Israel*, ed. H. G. M. Williamson (Oxford: Oxford University Press, 2007), 71–89; and John Van Seters, *In Search of History: Historiography in the Ancient World and the Origins of Biblical History* (New Haven: Yale University Press, 1983).

that uses the conventions, approaches, and principles of its ancient time and context. Biblical historical books communicated about events, people and interactions, dates and chronology, geographical and environmental factors, and causes and consequences, all in ways that made sense to their ancient audiences. Our procedure will be to provide quotes illustrative of history writing in the Bible and in the other cultures of that time that show how the biblical historical books display similar kinds of history writing within their broader context. This will help you to have an informed appreciation and understanding of how biblical history works. We will proceed by describing various characteristics of ancient history writing.

Chronological Structure

An initial characteristic of biblical history writing is that it constructs an account of the past that uses a chronological structure to organize the flow of the narrative. Like most histories, the historical books do try to relate the story of the past in some order like that in which events happened. Several aspects of the chronological flow of biblical history are important.

Much of the chronological ordering in the biblical historical books is conveyed by the narrative form of the story. As we saw in chapter 2, time sequencing creates an onward flow of the events, which conveys chronological time. However, chronology is also created by certain types of formulas that introduce narrative sections without specifying actual time periods. In the books of Joshua, 1 and 2 Samuel, and 1 Chronicles, short phrases such as "Now when all the kings heard . . ." or "Some time afterward . . ." are used in this way. The book of Judges is more explicit in giving chronology when it concludes the account of each judge's time as leader with a formula like "And the land had rest forty years" (Judg. 5:31). Another type of time phrase occurs in Ezra and Nehemiah where new incidents are sometimes marked by the day and/or month of the year in which an incident takes place, for example, "So the wall was finished on the twenty-fifth day of the month Ellul" (Neh. 6:15).

The most organized chronology occurs in the books that relate the reigns of the kings, 1 and 2 Kings and 2 Chronicles. We noted the brief introductions to each king's reign in two previous chapters because these regnal formulas both structure the narrative and convey the interests of the texts. These regnal formulas also give a highly structured chronology to these books. In the books of Kings, this chronology is complex because the text tracks the chronology of both Judah and Israel by overlapping the reigns of the kings, switching back and forth between the kingdoms, keeping both royal story lines simultaneously moving forward. Second Chronicles has a simpler format for its chronology because, as we saw above, it has no interest in tracking what is happening in Israel and only relates the chronology of the Judahite kings. It is interesting to note that if you tried to figure out the exact length and time of each king's reign or, even harder, tried to establish exactly how their reigns correspond to known events and kings in other ancient Near Eastern countries, your calculations would come up with several confusing details. Historians of ancient Israel and Judah have wrestled with the details of the given chronology,[8] but the point here is that the regnal markers convey a logical and generally chronological structure.

The chronological marking of kings' reigns is an aspect of the biblical historical books that is shared with the historiographies of its ancient neighbors. Kingdoms like Assyria and Babylon also kept various kinds of records about their kings that show a consistent concern to chronicle their kings, giving events by the year of the reign. Among the several types of ancient chronological texts, annals are lists that focus on royal names and reigns and sometimes add the kings' military campaigns. The brief style of such annals could be imaged as a "text message" that has a limited number of characters to convey information, so it is very compact, with each bit of writing summarizing a lot of actual information not included on the list. Consider this example from the Assyrian King Lists (material in brackets is restored by scholars):

8. For an excellent overview, see Marvin A. Sweeney, *I & II Kings: A Commentary*, Old Testament Library (Louisville: Westminster John Knox, 2007), 40–44.

Enlil-nasir, son of Puzur-Ashur, ruled for 13 years.

Nur-ili, son of Enlil-nasir, ruled for 12 years.

Ashur-shaduni, son of Nur-ili, ruled for 1 month.

Ashur-rabi, son of Enlil-nasir, ousted [Ashur-shaduni], seized the throne; [he ruled for x years].[9]

The format here is simple: the king's name, his father, and how long he reigned. However, even such a short form can be expanded to tell a bit of a story; if you read carefully you will see that an uncle ousted his nephew to seize the throne! The possibility of an annalistic record that correlates the reigns of kings in two neighboring countries, as is done in the Deuteronomistic History, is also supported by a document that lists the kings of Assyria and Babylon, adjoining states that sometimes shared a ruler. The Synchronistic Chronicle synchronizes the reigns by listing the kings of Assyria in one column and the corresponding rulers of Babylon in a second column.[10]

A longer form of record in the ancient world gives more information than the length of reign, with a broader focus on topics such as full military campaigns and battles, building projects, and religious actions like temple renovations.[11] This longer form appears in ancient Near Eastern inscriptions associated with building projects and in longer inscriptions or documents that cover a number of years. Here is an example of a chronicle entry about an Assyrian king from the eighth century BCE, which starts with the date of the month one king came to the throne: "On 27th Tebet Shalmaneser ascended the throne in Assyria and Babylon. He shattered Samaria. Year 5: Shalmaneser died in Tebet. Five years Shalmaneser ruled Babylonia

9. "Assyrian King Lists," ed. Alan Millard, in *The Context of Scripture*, ed. William Hallo, vol. 1, *Canonical Compositions from the Biblical World* (Leiden: Brill, 1997), 464.

10. "Babylonian and Assyrian Historical Texts," trans. A. Leo Oppenheim, in *Ancient Near Eastern Texts Relating to the Old Testament*, ed. James B. Pritchard, 3rd ed. (Princeton: Princeton University Press, 1969), 272–74.

11. Hayim Tadmor, "Autobiographical Apology in the Royal Assyrian Literature," in *History, Historiography and Interpretation: Studies in Biblical and Cuneiform Literatures*, ed. H. Tadmor and M. Weinfeld (Jerusalem: Magnes, 1983), 37.

and Assyria."[12] Another example comes from one of Judah and Israel's closest neighbors, the state of Moab. In an inscription carved on a black basalt stone, King Mesha (around 835 BCE) marked the building of a sanctuary ("high-place") for the god of Moab: "My father was king over Moab for thirty years, and I was king after my father. And I made this high-place for Kemosh."[13] The inscription goes on to give the king's description of some of the historical events leading up to the placing of the stone as a marker, showing how chronological notations are blended with longer texts in inscriptions (we will look at this again below).

Regnal formulas in the books of Kings sometimes give types of information similar to the annals and chronicles of these other states, citing reigns, battles, monumental building projects, and the establishment or renewal of sanctuaries: "In the thirty-first year of King Asa of Judah, Omri began to reign over Israel; he reigned for twelve years, six of them in Tirzah. He bought the hill of Samaria from Shemer for two talents of silver; he fortified the hill, and called the city that he built, Samaria, after the name of Shemer, the owner of the hill" (1 Kings 16:23–24). In fact, the biblical historical books clearly are familiar with the format of annals and chronicles and explicitly cite them as sources for the material about the kings. For example, one of the thirty-four such citations in the books of Kings reads, "The rest of the deeds of Hezekiah, all his power, how he made the pool and the conduit and brought water into the city, are they not written in the Book of the Annals of the Kings of Judah?" (2 Kings 20:20). There is more variety among the twenty-one citations of records like annals and chronicles in the books of Chronicles, including citations of prophetic records, as in the following example: "Now the acts of Rehoboam, from first to last, are they not written in the records of the prophet Shemaiah and of the seer Iddo, recorded by genealogy? There were continual wars between

12. "The Babylonian Chronicle," ed. Alan Millard, in Hallo, *Context of Scripture*, 1:467.
13. "The Inscription of King Mesha," ed. K. A. D. Smelik, in *The Context of Scripture*, ed. William Hallo, vol. 2, *Monumental Inscriptions from the Biblical World* (Leiden: Brill, 2000), 137.

Rehoboam and Jeroboam" (2 Chron. 12:15).[14] These citations of archival records, annals, and chronicles at the end of many sections on the kings' reigns function to validate the information the text has included by suggesting a knowledgeable source. They also imply that there is more information available, carefully chronicled by the royal scribes.

As a final feature of ancient chronicles, it is significant that in ancient Near Eastern texts, chronicles can cover extended periods of time. The Assyrian King Lists cited above recreate a line of about fourteen hundred years of royal reigns. The Babylonian Chronicles, some copies written on long tablets, include one version that contains entries about Assyrian and Babylonian kings covering over five hundred years.[15] As a modern parallel, you might think of a series of Facebook postings from a movie star or media-savvy politician who consistently posts comments about their daily activities—if you collected all the postings you might have several years of their daily notes about their public activities. The long view of royal reigns and actions seen in ancient Near Eastern chronicles is also paralleled in the biblical historical books: the Deuteronomistic History relates stories encompassing about six hundred years, Chronicles about four hundred years, and Ezra-Nehemiah about one hundred to one hundred fifty years.

Narrative Content

A second characteristic of biblical history writing is that while chronology gives structure, the content added to the chronology is in a narrative format using story-type elements to create the text. You may have noticed that for each chronological section in biblical historical books, the narrative that follows a chronological marker

14. For discussion of the sources mentioned in Chronicles, see Sara Japhet, *I & II Chronicles: A Commentary*, Old Testament Library (Louisville: Westminster John Knox, 1993), 14–23.

15. Meindert Dijkstra, "'As for the Other Events . . .': Annals and Chronicles in Israel and the Ancient Near East," in *The Old Testament in Its World*, ed. R. P. Gordon and J. C. deMoor (Leiden: Brill, 2005), 24–25.

is given in the form of stories that vary in length depending on how much material is included for the character or time period introduced. In some cases, only a very small bit of story line is included—for example, just two verses for the judge Tola (Judg. 10:1–2) and three verses for King Elah of Israel (1 Kings 16:8–10). By contrast, King Ahab of Israel receives six and a half chapters of material in the "window" opened on his reign (1 Kings 16:29–22:40), and, as we noted in chapter 3, David's story is related in sixty-one chapters. Such a weight of material on someone like Ahab or David makes each king more present in the text, and this conveys that the historical writing takes more interest in their impact on the history related. But it is story that makes up the content.

Scholars who study the field of historiography have noted that writing about the past very often takes the form of narrative or story. This may be so because the past *itself* actually has the shape of narrative or story, or the widespread use of narrative form may simply be because the past is remembered through the human capacity to make and understand stories. These issues are matters of debate.[16] Further, use of a narrative format need not imply that the past being remembered is "made up" or fictional; rather, the story format conveys the meaning of the past in a way understandable for an audience.[17] For example, narrative qualities allow the past to be described and interpreted in ways that a listing of dates and people in annals or simple chronicles misses. Connections between events, insights into the character of persons in the story, descriptions and details of scenes and objects, focus on certain events or people or time periods while leaving out others—all these facets of storytelling are crucial to the construction of a historical narrative that makes sense of the past.[18] Think of the common essay students are asked to write every fall: "What I Did on My Summer Vacation." Rarely do students just list dates in these essays; rather, they usually tell

16. V. Philips Long, "History and Fiction: What Is History?," in Long, *Israel's Past in Present Research*, 241–43.
17. Ferdinand Deist, "Contingency, Continuity and Integrity in Historical Understanding," in Long, *Israel's Past in Present Research*, 385.
18. Long, "History and Fiction," 245.

stories about their summer that reveal what they enjoyed or what they perhaps learned about themselves or what they really hated about that awful camp experience.

The recognition that history writing uses a story format to tell about the past is significant for our study because this trait can be seen in the historiography of the ancient world, including the biblical historical books. In chapter 2 we looked in detail at how biblical storytelling works, so we will not repeat that focus here. Rather, we will briefly show how a number of the cultures of the ancient world also related the past in the form of more extended accounts that have story elements, where a fuller description of events, people, places, connections between incidents, and causes of events have been included within the chronological structure. A modern example might be a document created by a family tracing their ancestry with information compiled from websites that can cover numerous entries and incidents over hundreds of years. Many dates and individual names would probably be included, but the family researcher would also include any stories found about ancestors, particularly the interesting or colorful characters who inhabit family histories. The family historian might add comments that draw connections between ancestors and current family members, or explain why a family group emigrated from another country, or show how the included stories give insights into the family's background and identity. These kinds of additions to lists of dates and names make the history into a narrative that in turn makes sense to the family.

Many of the records we have from the ancient societies that surrounded Israel and Judah are cast in the form of chronicles that have minimal narrative format. However, even a chronicle format can include narrative elements to fill in the list of dates and events. Consider this entry from the Babylonian Chronicle, a chronological record of kings of Babylon:

> [Year 21:] the king of Babylon was in his country. Nebuchadrezzar, his eldest son, the crown prince, [called] out the [army of Babylon], took the van [vanguard] and went to Carchemish on the bank of the Euphrates. He crossed the river [to face the army of Egypt] which

was camped at Carchemish. [. . .] they fought together and the army of Egypt fled before him. He defeated them utterly.[19]

However, the presentation of an account in narrative form in ancient records can be much more thorough so that the text reads fully like a story. An Egyptian text will provide an illustration of the possibilities of such extended narrative formats in ancient history writing. Pharaoh Ramses II, who lived from 1301 to 1234 BCE, left long texts about the events and accomplishments of his reign on the walls of temples to celebrate his power. In the self-aggrandizing style of most ancient royal texts, these inscriptions tell of years of military exploits. One campaign against the Hittites was concluded by a treaty that created an alliance between the two countries, including the marriage of a Hittite princess to the pharaoh. Note the narrative mode in which the text describes this event mixed in with the chronological marker.

> Now after [many days they] reached (the city) Ramses Meri-Amon . . . and we celebrated the great marvels of valor and victory in the year 34, 3rd month of the second season. Then they ushered the daughter of the Great Prince of Hatti, who had come marching to Egypt, into the presence of his majesty, with very great tribute following her, without limit. . . . Then [his] majesty saw that she was fair of face [like] a goddess. . . . So she was beautiful in the heart of his majesty, and he loved her more than anything, as a good fortune for him.[20]

You see here how the text gives sympathetic detail about the princess and an interior view of her effect on Ramses II as a character, a narrative technique in the historical recollection.

From the Assyrian Empire, in addition to many chronicle-style historical inscriptions on monuments and in building foundations, some longer texts of historical writing have been discovered. One text, called the Apology of Esarhaddon, is a justification of this king's unusual succession to the throne, because his older brothers

---

19. "Babylonian Chronicle," 1:467–68.
20. "Egyptian Historical Texts," trans. John A. Wilson, in Pritchard, *Ancient Near Eastern Texts*, 258.

objected to him as a younger son inheriting the kingship. Written in the first-person voice, the usual style in which Assyrian royal scribes recorded texts for their king, the Apology describes vividly Esarhaddon's fight against his brothers.

> In front of me, . . . all their (i.e., the brothers') best soldiers blocked the advance of my expeditionary corps, sharpening their weapons (for the battle). But the terror (-inspiring) sight of the great gods, my lords, overwhelmed them and they turned into madmen when they saw the attack of my strong battle array. . . . But they, the usurpers, who had started the rebellion, deserted their (most) trustworthy troops, when they heard the approach of my expeditionary corps and fled to an unknown country.[21]

Replacing the dry manner of chronicles with strong description and detail, this text reads like the plot of an ancient action movie, even while it tells about the battle and legitimizes the power of the king. The past is recounted in the format of a narrative that helps the text convey its interests in that past. We saw in chapter 2 how this aspect of history writing is thoroughly present in biblical narrative.

Use of Past Traditions and Archives as Sources

The next characteristic of ancient history writing we will examine is the use of sources. You are familiar with the use of sources via quotes and footnotes in history books, journal articles, or Wikipedia entries where the writers base their research on primary sources as much as possible—documents, archaeological remains, archival data, diaries, eyewitness accounts, and so on, from the era about which they are writing. Secondary sources are documents created through the use of primary sources, often after the events of the time period are over. They function in a number of ways: they contain reports about the time period gleaned from primary sources, include summary or analytical material about the relevant time period, or refer

21. "Babylonian and Assyrian Historical Texts," 289–90.

to insights of persons contemporary with the relevant period that complement and extend the primary sources. Often, a new insight into a past event is achieved when a previously undiscovered primary source is published by a historian. Without such primary sources and secondary sources the writing of history would be difficult for recent time periods and nearly impossible for the past beyond the living memory of the writer and his or her contemporaries.

We discussed above how the careful and critical use and evaluation of sources is one of the marks of modern critical historical scholarship. We also saw that during most of the ancient period that encompassed biblical historical writing, historiography did not evidence this kind of critical evaluation of sources. However, ancient history writers did use sources in ways that worked for their recounting of the past. They did not use anything as modern as footnotes, of course, but in some cases they did acknowledge the source of their material. In other cases, their sources are unacknowledged, but there are enough surviving texts from some ancient societies to be able sometimes to reconstruct what they used as sources.

Let us look first at texts in biblical history writing that may well have sources that recount older traditions or previously composed accounts of the past. The most obvious text that used a previous account is Chronicles, which used the Deuteronomistic History as one of its sources, and we can compare the two histories side by side to see how the source was used.[22] Further, above we gave examples of another type of obvious citation of sources in the numerous references to the "chronological annals" or "chronicles" made in the biblical history books. Many scholars have argued that other sections of these books also have independent sources underlying them. In general, however, since in almost every case we do not have independent verification of the existence of such sources, scholars must make judgments about biblical sources from their knowledge of (1) the types of records and resources that have been discovered

---

22. John C. Endres, William R. Millar, and John Barclay Burns, *Chronicles and Its Synoptic Parallels in Samuel, Kings and Related Biblical Texts* (Collegeville, MN: Liturgical Press, 1998).

in other ancient states and (2) the types of oral information, like oral histories, genealogies, and legends, that similar nonliterate societies have used as forms of history telling. Several examples of probable sources in the historical books will illustrate.

There are sections of the historical books that seem to preserve the memory of early traditions about leaders and charismatic individuals who played roles in the formation of the political and religious institutions in various eras of the story of Israel and Judah. Recalling earlier tales or events in an ongoing story line is familiar from modern blockbuster movie series where a story takes three or more movies to recount, like the Harry Potter movies or the Batman Dark Knight trilogy. In the later movies, the directors will use dialogue or flashbacks or dream sequences to remind viewers about earlier parts of the story. In biblical history writing, such previous tales are included within the overall story. For example, in the book of Judges, there are stories about military deliverers and local tribally based leaders that likely preserve early materials used as sources for the account of the development of the communities that would become Israel and Judah.[23] The beginning of one account of an early leader begins, "At that time Deborah, a prophetess, wife of Lappidoth, was judging Israel. She used to sit under the palm of Deborah between Ramah and Bethel in the hill country of Ephraim; and the Israelites came up to her for judgment" (Judg. 4:4–5). Other types of early texts also probably stem from originally independent sources; for example, a poem preserved in Judges 5 gives another version of the story in which Deborah is a leader. This text is considered to be a very early poem celebrating a victory of some of the tribes against a Canaanite city-state.[24]

> The peasantry prospered in Israel,
>   they grew fat on plunder,
> because you arose, Deborah,
>   arose as a mother in Israel. . . .

23. J. Clinton McCann, *Judges*, Interpretation (Louisville: Westminster John Knox, 2002), 6.

24. Ibid., 55.

> To the sound of musicians at the watering places,
>   there they repeat the triumphs of the LORD,
>   the triumphs of his peasantry in Israel.
>
> Judges 5:7, 11

Likewise, in the books of Kings, there are a number of stories about prophets in interaction with other characters in the text, especially kings, which likely originated in stories about the prophets of that era. For the prophets Elijah and Elisha, these stories fit into the various "windows" opened for the reigns of kings Ahab, Ahaziah, Jehoram, and Jehu of Israel. The following brief tale is typical:

> A man came from Baal-shalishah, bringing food from the first fruits to the man of God: twenty loaves of barley and fresh ears of grain in his sack. Elisha said, "Give it to the people and let them eat." But his servant said, "How can I set this before a hundred people?" So he repeated, "Give it to the people and let them eat, for thus says the LORD, 'They shall eat and have some left.'" He set it before them, they ate, and had some left, according to the word of the LORD. (2 Kings 4:42–44)

These stories about the work and words of the prophets may well originate in an independent cycle of tales kept alive in oral traditions about prophetic actions. One such group of tales might have focused on royal military interventions and warfare; another oral tradition might have recalled prophetic interventions with the poor where the prophets' actions provide compassion, provisions, and survival for the vulnerable.[25] The folkloristic elements that we might consider miraculous and legendary can also be viewed as acts of power often found in oral tales in nonliterate societies. The memory of these acts of power helps the text convey the impact of prophetic word and authority through the events the story is remembering.

Other sources that seem to lie behind the text of the historical books stem from what could be official or archival records kept

25. J. Maxwell Miller and John H. Hayes, *A History of Ancient Israel and Judah*, 2nd ed. (Louisville: Westminster John Knox), 287.

by groups of scribes attached to the royal household or temple. The royal house and the temple in ancient terms were the government agencies that kept archives and records. Today, a blogger who wanted to make a point about what a celebrity did recently might include information from the Facebook postings by that person. For a biblical example, the story of Solomon's reign includes a list that might have come from an archive of officials who were in charge of procuring provisions for the king's household (which, as we saw in chap. 1, refers to the entire royal and military administration): "Solomon had twelve officials over all Israel, who provided food for the king and his household; each one had to make provision for one month in the year" (1 Kings 4:7). And in 1 Chronicles we read a list of officials who administered the king's property, which names a number of types of administrators, including, "Over the herds that pastured in Sharon was Shitrai the Sharonite. Over the herds in the valleys was Shaphat son of Adlai. . . . All these were stewards of King David's property" (1 Chron. 27:29, 31). Some scholars have proposed that these types of royal administrative lists are records contemporaneous with David and Solomon, and others hold that they reflect a later time period, but in any case such lists probably are independent records from within official circles that were taken up into the writing of the biblical text.[26]

Another type of biblical source that appears to be originally independent of the narrative is that of a genealogical or other list of persons. We described in chapter 3 how a list creates focus in a narrative by giving details and functions to create order and control. Two examples will illustrate lists that might have originated independently of the biblical historical book in which they are included. The first example is from a genealogical record: "The sons of Jerahmeel, the firstborn of Hezron: Ram his firstborn, Bunah, Oren, Ozem, and Ahijah. Jerahmeel also had another wife, whose name was Atarah; she was the mother of Onam. The sons of Ram, the firstborn of Jerahmeel: Maaz, Jamin, and Eker" (1 Chron. 2:25–27). And the second example is apparently from a military record: "The

---

26. For discussion, see Sweeney, *I & II Kings*, 89, and Japhet, *I & II Chronicles*, 472.

sons of Benjamin: Bela, Becher, and Jediael, three. The sons of Bela: Ezbon, Uzzi, Uzziel, Jerimoth, and Iri, five, heads of ancestral houses, mighty warriors; and their enrollment by genealogies was twenty-two thousand thirty-four" (1 Chron. 7:6–7). Such records might have been kept officially by the temple or by family or military groups. They are reported by Chronicles as a part of the text's focus on genealogical records, which helped establish the origin and identity of the people of the reconstituted community after the exile.[27]

Biblical history writing that emerged in the postexilic era in the books of Ezra and Nehemiah is more overt about showing the use of sources. We saw in chapter 3 how Ezra's mandate to establish the administration of Judah was reinforced by an authority argument created by the inclusion of quotes from a letter from the Persian king. Later the story is even more explicit about the existence and use of documents to make points about the course of events. The story relates that when opposition arose from factions resistant to the reestablishment of the temple in Jerusalem, both the Jewish authorities and their opponents appealed to the Persians to check the documentary record of the empire to support their opinion. The following text quotes from a letter of inquiry and the Persian king's reply:

> "And now, if it seems good to the king, have a search made in the royal archives there in Babylon, to see whether a decree was issued by King Cyrus for the rebuilding of this house of God in Jerusalem. Let the king send us his pleasure in this matter." Then King Darius made a decree, and they searched the archives where the documents were stored in Babylon. But it was in Ecbatana, the capital in the province of Media, that a scroll was found on which this was written: "A record. In the first year of his reign, King Cyrus issued a decree: Concerning the house of God at Jerusalem, let the house be rebuilt." (Ezra 5:17–6:3)

Turning to the neighbors of Israel and Judah, there is evidence in surviving texts that the writing of historical accounts in Assyria,

27. Japhet, *I & II Chronicles*, 19, 69, 169.

Writing Materials in the Ancient Near East

How was writing actually done by the scribes of the ancient Near Eastern societies we are studying? A variety of writing materials and techniques were used,[a] depending on the use intended:

- Stone, incised with a chisel: inscriptions and symbols on walls, pillars, monuments, and doorways; for public royal, military, and religious declarations and dedications
- Stone covered with plaster, inked with a brush: images, symbols, and inscriptions on walls, doorways, individual pieces of stone; for religious texts, blessings, records, and declarations
- Metal, incised with a stylus: images, symbols, and inscriptions on bronze, copper, or silver sheets or scrolls, or bronze weapons; for identification, or royal and religious texts and documents
- Pottery, inked with a brush or incised with a stylus: images, symbols, and inscriptions on pottery shard (ostracon) or whole vessel; for decoration, lists, letters, and records for accounting and trade
- Clay, impressions made by metal seal or incised with a stylus: symbols and inscriptions on jars, jar handles, letter seals, decorative objects; for decoration, lists, letters, and records for accounting and trade
- Leather, inked with a brush: on tanned animal hides and scrolls; inscriptions for texts, royal documents, letters, and religious documents
- Wood, wax covered, inscribed with a stylus: inscriptions, lists, and longer documents for letters and records
- Papyrus, inked with a brush: inscriptions, lists, and longer documents for letters, records, and religious texts

a. Philip J. King and Lawrence E. Stager, "Literacy and Schools," in *Life in Biblical Israel*, Library of Ancient Israel (Louisville: Westminster John Knox, 2001), 300–317.

Hatti, and Babylon also used as sources other texts, inscriptions, annals, and chronicles. For example, enough historical records from the Neo-Assyrian Empire survive to show that when a new chronicle or monumental inscription was needed to bring a king's achievements up to date, previous written records were used as sources, then

supplemented, embellished, and expanded in the new inscription.[28]
One scholar notes that ancient texts used as sources other historical
source materials like "annals, astronomical diaries and historical
chronicles."[29] A modern example might be a student who is trying
to get a loan from a bank for school. To convince the loan officer at
the bank that the student is creditworthy, the student has to produce
documents that give evidence of employment, current status as a
student, and perhaps parental support—these are all the student's
"sources" to make a convincing argument to the bank.

In ancient history writing, we have a good example from the
Hittite Old Kingdom (about 1300 BCE). A document from there
explicitly speaks of the search for historical records and includes an
extended summary from one of the records it cites. The situation
behind the Plague Prayers of King Muršili II apparently was an
extended plague that had been brought to his land by prisoners of
war captured in a battle some twenty years previously. The king in
the prayers recorded in the texts is appealing for help from the gods
to end the plague by seeking the cause of the divine disfavor that
has caused the plague to break out. One recorded prayer includes
the following:

> [I sought (the cause of) the anger] of the gods, [and I found] two old
> tablets. One tablet [dealt with the ritual. . . .] . . . The second tablet
> dealt with . . . {the following} although the Hittites and the Egyptians
> {in a dispute at that time} had been put under oath by the Storm-god
> of Hatti . . . the Hittites transgressed the oath. . . . When I found
> the tablet mentioned earlier dealing with Egypt, I made an oracular
> inquiry of a god about it. . . . It was ascertained (through an oracle)
> that the cause of the anger of the Storm-god of Hatti was . . . the
> Hittites on their own suddenly transgressed the word (of the oath).[30]

This citation of a source is even more interesting in that the same
source, the "old tablet" about the Storm-god, is referred to in

28. Tadmor, "Autobiographical Apology," 46.
29. Dijkstra, "'As for the Other Events,'" 23.
30. "Plague Prayers of Muršili II," ed. Gary Beckman, in Hallo, *Context of Scripture*, 1:158.

another Hittite historical record, the Deeds of Šuppiluliuma, for a different purpose.[31] This example predates, but shows a similar attitude toward, the use of explicit mention of a source document in the account noted above from Ezra. In a very different world and context from our own, ancients apparently saw the utility of referring to their sources when undertaking different types of historical writing.

A Greek historian from a much later period can also provide an example of the use of an independent source in constructing a historical report. Herodotus, in writing his account of the Persian Empire, reports the following about King Darius's actions after he came to the throne: "Darius . . . divided his dominions into twenty governments, called by the Persians satrapies; and . . . ordained that each several nation should pay him tribute."[32] In reporting the satrapy system, Herodotus probably used a Persian source for his detailed description of the Persian provinces and their taxation duties.[33]

As we noted in the introduction to this chapter, the Greek writers made extensive use of their own first-person accounts and eyewitness accounts of others in relating the events in their histories. However, the Greeks also collected tales from either the places they visited or the informers with whom they spoke, and their sources included these tales. Herodotus, for example, reports one tale with a note about its probability.

> I must relate the less credible tale also, since [the Arabians] tell it. There is a great river in Arabia called Corys, issuing into the sea called Red. From this river (it is said) the kind of the Arabians carried water by a duct of sewn ox-hides and other hides of length sufficient to reach the dry country and he had great tanks dug in that country to receive and keep the water. It is a twelve days journey from the river to that country.[34]

31. Hans G. Güterbock, "Hittite Historiography: A Survey," in Tadmor and Weinfeld, *History, Historiography and Interpretation*, 32.

32. Herodotus, *Histories* 3.89, in *Herodotus*, trans. A. D. Godley, Loeb Classical Library (London: William Heinemann, 1929), 2:117.

33. Momigliano, *Classical Foundations*, 13.

34. Herodotus, *Histories* 3.9 (trans. Godley, 2:13).

As we have seen, all these ancient societies included sources of various kinds in their historical writing, whether they acknowledged the sources or not. In this regard, biblical historical writing is typical of its context.

Use of Direct Speech

A final category of source in all these types of ancient history writing is problematic for modern readers but was apparently an accepted and usual convention for the writers from those ancient centuries and cultures. This category is the use of direct speech, often appearing as if it were a quote from one or more characters in the account. A modern example of a similar use of direct speech in a historical format would be the dialogue created for a movie that recreates a historical event. A documentary about an event in American history may not have historical documentation for everything that the characters in the movie say, but the film's writer and director re-create realistic and reasonable dialogue for the characters.

The biblical historical books made wide use of this convention of inserting speeches by characters in their accounts. For example, speeches are reported that come from public events like the dedication of the temple related during Solomon's reign.

> Then Solomon stood before the altar of the LORD in the presence of all the assembly of Israel, and spread out his hands to heaven. He said, "O LORD, God of Israel, there is no God like you in heaven above or on earth beneath, keeping covenant and steadfast love for your servants who walk before you with all their heart." (1 Kings 8:22–23)

In the case of a quote from a public event, it could be argued that witnesses to or memories of the event recalled the speech or prayer. However, biblical history writers also insert quotes from a wide variety of characters, including enemy kings, commanders, and servants, that would not have been public events, as least for Judah and Israel. In a story about a war between Israel and the Arameans, the text reports a conversation between the Aramean king and his servants.

The servants of the king of Aram said to him, "Their gods are
gods of the hills, and so they were stronger than we; but let us fight
against them in the plain, and surely we shall be stronger than they
. . . and muster an army like the army that you have lost, horse
for horse, and chariot for chariot; then we will fight against them
in the plain, and surely we shall be stronger than they." He heeded
their voice, and did so. (1 Kings 20:23, 25)

Biblical historical texts also report conversations that are conveyed as private words between two characters or words spoken by
one character when alone. For example, when Elisha is confronted
with the death of a child of a widow whom he had previously
helped, he takes the child to an upper room and then prays. The
story quotes his prayer, said when he was alone in the room: "He
cried out to the LORD, 'O LORD my God, have you brought calam-
ity even upon the widow with whom I am staying, by killing her
son?'" (1 Kings 17:20).

Finally, words from God are reported either as direct speech to
a character or through the agency of a prophet who has heard the
words and then reports them to the proper recipient. At one point,
1 Chronicles reports a conversation between God and David, when
David's forces were threatened by the Philistines: "David inquired
of God, 'Shall I go up against the Philistines? Will you give them
into my hand?' The LORD said to him, 'Go up, and I will give them
into your hand'" (1 Chron. 14:10).

This same type of inserted speech is common in the texts from
Israel and Judah's ancient neighbors. "While the use of direct speech
is not acceptable in today's modern canon of history writing un-
less it is a quote, in ancient history writing direct speech was quite
common."[35] Of all the types of history writing we have reviewed
for this chapter, only Thucydides, a history writer from the developing analytical tradition in Greece, reports trying to keep close
to the sense of what a speaker actually said.[36] Most ancient texts,
however, just insert speech from a wide variety of persons in various

35. Younger, "Underpinnings," 317.
36. Ibid.

circumstances. Some texts report speeches that are either attributed
or conveyed as public acts and so might come from a memory of
an event. An example comes from the reign of Ramses II of Egypt.

> Words spoken by his majesty: "As my father Re favors me forever
> as Ruler of the Two Lands, as I rise like the sun disc and shine
> like Re, as the heaven is firm upon its supports, I will attain the
> limits of the land of Hatti, and they shall be prostrate under my
> feet forever."[37]

Other texts include speech that comes from sources and people
not in the immediate circle of the writers. One Hittite text quotes
the enemies who are planning to attack a new king of Hatti. "The
enemy in foreign lands said as follows: 'His father, who was king of
Hatti, was a heroic king. . . . Now the one who has sat down on his
father's throne is a child. He will not (be able to) save the borders of
Hatti and Hatti itself.'"[38] The Mesha inscription, cited above, also
quotes an enemy, though in this case the enemy quoted is a king of
Israel, one of Omri's heirs on the throne.

> Omri was the king of Israel,
> and he oppressed Moab for many days . . .
> And his son succeeded him,
> And he said—he too—
> "I will oppress Moab!"[39]

The same inscription of King Mesha also includes another typical
quote used in ancient sources: a quote from a god, in this case the
god Kemosh of Moab:

> And Kemosh said to me:
> "Go, take Nebo from Israel!"[40]

37. "Egyptian Historical Texts," 257.
38. "The Ten Year Annals of Great King Muršili II of Hatti," ed. Richard H. Beal,
in Hallo, *Context of Scripture*, 2:84.
39. "Inscription of King Mesha," 2:137.
40. Ibid., 2:138.

In the religious systems of the ancient Near East, words from the gods could be obtained through religious rituals like prayer or the reading of various omens when the god's will was sought by a priest or religious functionary, or through the words given by a prophet. The text of the document in which Esarhaddon, king of Assyria, justifies his place on the throne, quotes from the gods:

> I prayed to Ashur, Sin, Shamash, Bel, Nebo, and Nergal, (to) Ishtar of Ninevah, the Ishtar of Arbela and they agreed to give an (oracle-) answer . . . they sent me the (following) trustworthy oracle . . . "Go (ahead), do not tarry! We will march with you, kill your enemies!"[41]

All these examples of inserted speech events help convey the sense of the past that is being communicated by the ancient texts. The conventions of ancient history writing allowed texts simply to insert the speeches as they fit the account being related. This aspect of ancient writing can be appreciated as apparently making sense in its context because it is so widely used in ancient writing. Further, it is also possible to see how particular speeches help the texts convey their interests, a topic we have noted before. Where a king reports that a god has spoken to him to give direction about a battle or building a sanctuary, that quote is supporting the claim of the king to be doing the god's will. Where a text inserts a speech by a leading figure, the speech functions as part of the overall impact of the story being related.

Conclusion

The characteristics of ancient history writing that we have examined in this chapter all help that writing to convey its account of what took place in the past. Using a chronological structure and a narrative content help order these ancient accounts so that they made sense as story lines. We have also seen how historical accounts from both the Bible and other ancient societies use sources of various kinds:

41. "Babylonian and Assyrian Historical Texts," 289.

past traditions and previous accounts of events; legends and cycles
of tales about heroes, prophets, and warriors; and archives and lists.
Finally, we saw how ancient history writing inserts quotes from
major figures in the account being related and how that adds impact
and liveliness to the tale being recounted. All these elements help to
turn the accounts into more than lists of dates and names. Indeed,
these elements make the account of the past read like an interesting
story that helps the historian communicate to their audience. We
will see in the next chapter that ancient history writers also took
care to shape how they were telling about the past. The accounts are
shaped through techniques like selectivity and evaluation; this also
makes an impact on an audience to guide what is related about the
past. Those history-writing techniques used by ancient texts will
be our final exploration for reading biblical history.

Suggested Reading

Gordon, R. P., and J. C. deMoor, eds. *The Old Testament in Its World*.
Leiden: Brill, 2005.

Hallo, William, ed. *The Context of Scripture*. Vol. 1, *Canonical Compositions from the Biblical World*. Vol. 2, *Monumental Inscriptions from the Biblical World*. Vol. 3, *Archival Documents from the Biblical World*.
Leiden: Brill, 1997–2002.

Long, V. Philips, ed. *Israel's Past in Present Research: Essays on Ancient Israelite Historiography*. Winona Lake, IN: Eisenbrauns, 1999.

Machinist, Peter. "The Voice of the Historian in the Ancient Near East and Mediterranean World." *Interpretation* 57 (2003): 117–37.

Moore, Megan Bishop, and Brad E. Kelle. *Biblical History and Israel's Past: The Changing Study of the Bible and History*. Grand Rapids and Cambridge: Eerdmans, 2011.

Pritchard, James B., ed. *Ancient Near Eastern Texts Relating to the Old Testament*. 3rd ed. Princeton: Princeton University Press, 1969.

Pury, Albert de, Thomas Römer, and Jean-Danel Macchi, eds. *Israel Constructs Its History: Deuteronomistic Historiography in Recent Research*.
Journal for the Study of the Old Testament Supplement Series 306.
Sheffield: Sheffield Academic Press, 2000.

Tadmor, Hayim, and Moshe Weinfeld, eds. *History, Historiography and Interpretation: Studies in Biblical and Cuneiform Literatures.* Jerusalem: Magnes, 1983.

Van Seters, John. *In Search of History: Historiography in the Ancient World and the Origins of Biblical History.* New Haven: Yale University Press, 1983.

Williamson, H. G. M, ed. *Understanding the History of Ancient Israel.* Oxford: Oxford University Press, 2007.

Discussion Questions

1. If you remembered a family story or memoir (in the discussion questions for the introduction and chap. 1), go back to that story again. What elements about it are conveyed as a narrative? What sources does the story refer to or include, like photographs, a family Bible, or birth or baptism certificates? If you went to an ancestry database on the web, what sources might you find there that would give further information about your family story?

2. One aspect of the narrative structure of history writing in the Bible is that even nonnarrative formats are made part of the story; for example, law codes or lists are included as speeches given by a major character rather than simply arranged as an independent section. What do you think is the effect of subsuming all the sources, incidents, and formats under the rubric of storytelling?

3. What are the effects on your interpretation of the text when you understand the biblical narrative's inclusion of quotes from characters that are otherwise not verifiable?

5

Examining the Shape of History
in the Text

We now address characteristics of ancient history writing that have in a sense already been introduced: ancient historical writing demonstrates interests in how the past is narrated. As we examined in chapter 3, ancient texts show that they are not trying to present neutral observations of events but rather trying to communicate particular interests through the story they relate. As examples of history writing, both biblical texts and other ancient Near Eastern texts shape how the story of the past is conveyed in a variety of ways so that the audience is left with a particular picture of the past. You are familiar already from your own life with this shaping of an account of the past. You might imagine teenagers recounting the story of the previous night's party to minimize their own role in the mess that was left behind. Or, more significantly, you might imagine a community youth group telling the tale of their volunteer work with a neighborhood organization that was helping to clean up a local park by highlighting the importance of their tasks in the overall effort. These kinds of accounts are shaped to have an effect on what the audience of the story thinks about the past that is related. This chapter will explore how this shaping of the past worked in ancient history writing.

Shaping the Story of the Past: Selectivity

Every writer of a historical account, even someone writing about what he or she did for summer vacation, has to practice selectivity— you cannot narrate every minute of your summer in one essay, so you select the highlights as you understand them and want to communicate them. You might include activities like the job that showed your responsibility and exclude some of the parties that were fun but might convey something you would rather keep private.

This first way in which ancient historical writing shaped the story of the past—through selectivity—builds immediately on the section in the previous chapter about the sources of the historical texts. It is clear in both biblical and other ancient writing that only particular sources were included, that is, that the writers of these texts were selective in how they used their sources. The selectivity of the biblical texts is both obvious and stated by the texts themselves. For example, the books of Chronicles do not include large sections of their source, the Deuteronomistic History—evidently because the focus of Chronicles on the Davidic monarchy and Judah made the stories about the northern kingdom irrelevant. We also have mentioned how the repeated references to annals and chronicles in the regnal formulas in Kings and Chronicles demonstrate that the text deliberately shows awareness that there were other stories that could have been included from such sources, but again, only the bits were included that fit the interests of the way the past was being recounted. Another way we can show that the biblical historical texts are selective in what they include comes from a study of inscriptions from the Neo-Assyrian Empire. In inscriptions from the time of Shalmaneser III, two events are recounted that mention the northern kingdom, Israel. One is a battle in 853 BCE that included forces from the Israelite state, and the other is the extraction of tribute from King Jehu of Israel by the Assyrians.[1] Neither event is mentioned in biblical historical texts, so evidently they were not selected for inclusion in the way the story was told about Israel.

In the societies contemporaneous with Israel and Judah, selectivity was also practiced in how the past was recounted. A broad review of many sources from these societies shows that historical writing focused on a select set of activities, most of them centered on central state institutions like the dynasty and administration, state and monumental building projects, tax and tribute systems, international relations with other states by conquest and alliance, and religious structures like temples, sanctuaries, offerings, and omens. Hittite inscriptions repeatedly address wars and expansion or development, building projects, religious and cult activities, royal family affairs and legitimacy of succession, actions of various officials, practices of rulers like the administration of justice, and curses against any who would damage the inscriptions.[2] The historical inscriptions and texts from the Assyrian Empire show a parallel focus on the king, which often takes the form of a listing of royal deeds, "narrating the achievements of the king as a military-hero and as a pious master-builder."[3] One scholar has noted that the action of selection of sources, among other activities in constructing a chronicle, is in fact one of the marks both of the chronicle form and of early history writing. "Chronicles are those texts that digest a selection of traditions, events, observations and other data in a chronographic structure and synthesise them into historiography. Interpreting those sources by selecting, summarising, revising and criticising from a

---

1. K. Lawson Younger Jr., "Neo-Assyrian and Israelite History," in *Understanding the History of Ancient Israel*, ed. H. G. M. Williamson (Oxford: Oxford University Press, 2007), 246.

2. Kenneth A. Kitchen, "The Hieroglyphic Inscriptions of the Neo-Hittite States (c. 1200–700 BC)," in *The Old Testament in Its World*, ed. R. P. Gordon and J. C. deMoor (Leiden: Brill, 2005), 117–34.

3. Hayim Tadmor, "Autobiographical Apology in the Royal Assyrian Literature," in *History, Historiography and Interpretation: Studies in Biblical and Cuneiform Literatures*, ed. H. Tadmor and M. Weinfeld (Jerusalem: Magnes, 1983), 37.

distance is the true mark of early historiography."[4] When we review
what ancient history writing did include we are reminded that, as in
biblical texts, the lives and concerns of common people are barely
visible, except perhaps indirectly as the victims or recipients of royal
attention, a quality we examined above.

Shaping the Story of the Past: Patterns and Causes

A major portion of the methods that ancient texts used to shape
the story of the past has to do with how they go beyond the dry
lists of people and events and the vast number of individual bits of
information available from their sources. What made the historical
writings more than a mere listing of events were the connections
drawn in the writings themselves through and over the structure of
chronology, the format of narrative, and the use of sources. Historical writings in the ancient world added shape to the past by
offering descriptions of patterns perceived in past events, providing
explanations of causes, presenting evaluation of events and persons,
and proposing interpretations of the past. These methods created
connections among bits of information that would otherwise be
random and by that showed how the past "makes sense." We will deal
with the first two methods in this section. You might keep in mind
how modern family historians might also begin to see patterns once
they have accumulated enough stories about their ancestors, perhaps
seeing that success in agriculture or trade ran in the family, or that
the women of the family tended to be particularly strong influences
on the choices that their families made. The family historian might
look for the causes that urged one generation to emigrate—a time
of famine, or hope for a better life or more freedom.

The description of patterns perceived in events was one sort of
ordering by which the past was shaped. A pattern creates order and
regularity in contrast to a recounting of unconnected events that may

---

4. Meindert Dijkstra, "'As for the Other Events . . .': Annals and Chronicles in
Israel and the Ancient Near East," in Gordon and deMoor, *The Old Testament in
Its World*, 25.

"Public" History

Some of the ancient "documents" that historians use to research the ancient Near East come in the form of monumental inscriptions—writing on building walls, city gates, doorways, monuments and obelisks, and temples. These inscriptions often served political or religious purposes, celebrating a king's victory over enemies or conquest of territory, proclaiming the state's controlling interests over vassals, or acknowledging the divine legitimacy of the royal house. Some of the most dramatic writings include:

Karnak, the temple complex at Thebes, Egypt, built in many phases over a 1,500-year period from about 1900 BCE to about 400 BCE. Many temples, courts, and pillars contain carved reliefs of royal and ritual scenes and hieroglyphic inscriptions; in particular the Hypostyle Hall built by pharaohs Sety I and Rameses II contains 134 huge stone columns up to 67 feet tall.[a]

The Black Obelisk, a black limestone pillar about 6.5 feet high, erected in 825 BCE by Assyrian king Shalmaneser III to celebrate his military victories. The inscriptions include carved pictures of conquered foreign kings bringing tribute to Shalmaneser and lists of the tribute amounts and types.[b]

The Behistun Relief, a huge relief (48 x 80 feet) that was carved into a rock wall three hundred feet above a major roadway during the reign of Darius I of Persia in 520 BCE. This gigantic advertisement for Darius's power and military victories shows him standing over his conquered rival, and a long inscription in three languages describes his victories.[c]

a. "Digital Karnak," *Digital Karnak Project*, University of California at Los Angeles, accessed December 30, 2012, http://dlib.etc.ucla.edu/projects/Karnak/.

b. "The Black Obelisk of Shalmaneser III," *British Museum*, accessed December 30, 2012, http://www.britishmuseum.org/explore/highlights/highlight_objects/me/t/black_obelisk_of_ shalmaneser.aspx.

c. "Bisotun," *UNESCO World Heritage Centre*, accessed December 30, 2012, http://whc.unesco.org /en/list/1222.

appear random or disorganized. In chapter 3 we saw how the interests of the text are conveyed in the creation of patterns. In biblical history writing, analogies and models are also ways the texts draw attention to connections among people and events. We have seen how the notation of chronology adds a repetitive outline for the past, especially where the regnal formulas create regularity in how each king is introduced and summarized. Beyond such a design for chronology, one prime example of a clear establishment of a pattern used to convey the meaning of past events is in the book of Judges. In Judges 2, the text provides a summary by which it shows a pattern of events that shapes the account of the time period as it follows in the book.

> Then the Israelites did what was evil in the sight of the LORD and worshiped the Baals; and they abandoned the LORD, the God of their ancestors, who had brought them out of the land of Egypt; they followed other gods, from among the gods of the peoples who were all around them, and bowed down to them; and they provoked the LORD to anger. . . . So the anger of the LORD was kindled against Israel, and he gave them over to plunderers who plundered them, and he sold them into the power of their enemies all around, so that they could no longer withstand their enemies. . . . [But when the Israelites cried out to the Lord (cf. 3:9)] the LORD raised up judges, who delivered them out of the power of those who plundered them. . . . Whenever the LORD raised up judges for them, the LORD was with the judge, and he delivered them from the hand of their enemies all the days of the judge; for the LORD would be moved to pity by their groaning because of those who persecuted and oppressed them. But whenever the judge died, they would relapse and behave worse than their ancestors, following other gods, worshiping them and bowing down to them. (Judg. 2:11–12, 14, 16, 18–19)

This pattern of unfaithfulness and abandoning God, suffering under enemies, crying out to God, receiving a divinely appointed judge deliverer, experiencing a period of peace under the judge, and then backsliding when the judge died is applied in much of the rest of the book. It structures the accounts of the judge deliverers, using repetition of the key phrases from the pattern. The model conveys the interests of the text as it profiles the tales in which the clans and tribes of the early community maintain faithfulness (or not) with the God who delivered them from Egypt.

The use of patterns to draw connections among events is also evident in the historical writing of the neighbors of Israel and Judah.

For example, a set of clay tablets from the Neo-Assyrian Empire dating to 842 BCE tells of the military campaigns of Shalmaneser III, first using a chronological patterning.

> In my sixth regnal year, I departed from Nineveh. . . . I entered the city of Tīl-turaḫi. I claimed the city as my own. . . .

> In my tenth regnal year, I crossed the Euphrates for the eighth time. I razed, destroyed, (and) burned the cities of Sangara, the Carchemishite. . . .

> In my eleventh regnal year, I departed Nineveh. . . . I captured the city of Aštammaku together with 89 cities.[5]

After this chronological patterning, which structures the account of a number of years, the text concludes by giving a different pattern to the same events, this time in a geographical summary of the areas Shalmaneser conquered.

> I ruled over the land of Hatti in its entirety. I conquered from the source of the Tigris to the source of the Euphrates. I devastated like a flood from the land of Enzi to the land of Suḫni, from the land of Suḫni to the land of Melid, from the land of Melid to the land of Daiēnu, from the land of Daiēnu to the city of Arṣaškun.[6]

The use of both patterns in the same text conveys the clear interests of the inscription to present Shalmaneser III as the powerful conqueror of a vast area.

Another example of fashioning patterns in previous events is evident from the Ten Year Annals of the Hittite king Muršili. As the recounting of his military campaigns proceeds in these annals, a repeated phrase throughout the text draws a connection among all the battles that are represented as victories: "The Sun goddess

5. "Annals: Aššur Clay Tablets," ed. K. Lawson Younger Jr., in *The Context of Scripture*, ed. William Hallo, vol. 2, *Monumental Inscriptions from the Biblical World* (Leiden: Brill, 2000), 264–65.
6. Ibid., 2:265.

of Arinna, my lady, the victorious Stormgod, my lord, Mezulla and all the gods ran before me. I defeated . . ."[7] As we noted with the creation of patterns in the historical writing in the Bible, such patterns in the inscriptions and documents of the ancient Near East generate a way to perceive past events that are included in the patterns as well as to convey the interests of the texts.

Another technique by which ancient history writing gave shape to the past was by providing explanations of the causes of events. In this instance, the texts propose to look behind the events themselves to explain why things happened as they did. Almost universally throughout the ancient world of the time of biblical historical writing, the primary cause of events in the human world was understood to be the intervention, either directly or implicitly, of the divine world. Each nation understood in its own particular way that the god or gods to which they paid allegiance were responsible for the affairs of humanity. So in the historical writing we have explored, the direction and intervention of the gods is often expressed as a cause of the events related.

The writing of history in the Bible was no exception to this but of course found the course of human life and events to be under the providence of the God who had been the God of their ancestors. In various ways the texts express that when humans either did or did not pay attention to the values by which God expected humans to make choices and guide their behavior, consequences inherent in the behavior by God's intention played out. Sometimes the intervention of God is expressed explicitly—for example, that the choice of the dynasty that would rule the nation is under the Lord's guidance. As the tale is related in the Deuteronomistic History, when the first king, Saul, failed to live up to the standards revealed by the prophet Samuel, another king was chosen by God's direct intervention.

> Jesse made seven of his sons pass before Samuel, and Samuel said to Jesse, "The LORD has not chosen any of these." Samuel said to

7. "The Ten Year Annals of Great King Muršili II of Hatti," ed. Richard H. Beal, in Hallo, *Context of Scripture*, 2:84.

Jesse, "Are all your sons here?" And he said, "There remains yet the youngest, but he is keeping the sheep." And Samuel said to Jesse, "Send and bring him; for we will not sit down until he comes here." He sent and brought him in. Now he was ruddy, and had beautiful eyes, and was handsome. The LORD said, "Rise and anoint him; for this is the one." Then Samuel took the horn of oil, and anointed him in the presence of his brothers; and the spirit of the LORD came mightily upon David from that day forward. (1 Sam. 16:10–13)

In other cases, the consequences of human action are expressed as an inevitable outcome of human behavior. Among the numerous examples we could give, the following is one of the more explicit in a section of the Deuteronomistic History reflecting on the fall of Samaria, the capital city of Israel, to the Assyrian Empire:

In the ninth year of Hoshea the king of Assyria captured Samaria; he carried the Israelites away to Assyria. . . . This occurred because the people of Israel had sinned against the LORD their God, who had brought them up out of the land of Egypt from under the hand of Pharaoh king of Egypt. They had worshiped other gods and walked in the customs of the nations whom the LORD drove out before the people of Israel, and in the customs that the kings of Israel had introduced. (2 Kings 17:6–8)

These and other texts express not only that national and international relationships fell under the auspices of God but also that significant political changes were under God's implicit or explicit guidance. The clear theological interests of the texts come through in this attribution of causes.

The books of Chronicles contain the historical writing with the strongest sense of determination of events by God and a corollary principle, that the consequences of every deed are unfailingly determined by God's justice so that good is always rewarded and evil always punished. "Human act, good or evil, is always and immediately recompensed, and any human state of welfare or misfortune is a consequence of God's retribution, measured to fit the human conduct."[8] An example of God directing the punishment of a king for unfaithful behavior is found in the tale of King Joash. As Chronicles relates the account, this king had originally been faithful to God under the influence of the priest Jehoiada, but once the priest died, Joash turned away, and defeat in war was the consequence.

> Now after the death of Jehoiada the officials of Judah came and did obeisance to the king; then the king listened to them. They abandoned the house of the LORD, the God of their ancestors, and served the sacred poles and the idols. And wrath came upon Judah and Jerusalem for this guilt of theirs. . . . At the end of the year the army of Aram came up against Joash. . . . Although the army of Aram had come with few men, the LORD delivered into their hand a very great army, because they had abandoned the LORD, the God of their ancestors. Thus they executed judgment on Joash. (2 Chron. 24:17–18, 23–24)

The historical writing of other nations of the ancient Near East, focused as it was on military, dynastic, and cultic matters, also strongly expressed the intervention of the gods in the affairs of humans.[9] "Every war of Assyria, led by her monarch—and in theory the high priest of Ashur—was on a theological as well as on a practical-cultic level a 'holy war.'"[10] Another example is the Apology of Esarhaddon, which illustrates the divine election of an Assyrian king. In this case, claiming divine election was particularly important because he had come to the throne as a younger son, supplanting his older brothers. The inscription begins with these words:

> Property of Esarhaddon, great king, legitimate king, king of the world, king of Assyria, regent of Babylon, king of Sumer and Akkad, king of the four rims (of the earth), the true shepherd, favorite of the great gods, whom Ashur, Shamash, Bel and Nebo, the Ishtar of

8. Sara Japhet, "Postexilic Historiography: How and Why?," in *Israel Constructs Its History: Deuteronomistic Historiography in Recent Research*, ed. Albert de Pury et al., Journal for the Study of the Old Testament Supplement Series 306 (Sheffield: Sheffield Academic Press, 2000), 164.

9. Dijkstra, "'As for the Other Events,'" 18.

10. Tadmor, "Autobiographical Apology," 42.

Nineveh (and) the Ishtar of Arbela have pronounced king of Assyria (ever) since he was a youngster.[11]

Parallel to the principles of thought about divine intervention in all ancient historical writing, actions and situations in the historiography of a nation like Moab could also be attributed to causes such as the anger of their god Kemosh. These lines come from the inscription by King Mesha of Moab, giving a historical view of the relationship between Moab and Israel under King Omri:

> Omri was the king of Israel,
> And he oppressed Moab for many days,
> For Kemosh was angry with his land.[12]

While much of the historical writing of the ancient Near East, including biblical historiography, attributed causality for human events and situations to the gods, we also find expressions of causes that reflect the intentions and motivations of purely human actors. Apparently, causality could be found in both divine and human will within the theological thought of each society. You are probably most familiar with the identification of this type of cause in contemporary history writing. For example, a history of a particular region of the country may trace how economic tensions with a neighboring region caused changes in political agendas. The historian in this case is looking at how the workings of human decision making changed the course of events.

We will start with indications in biblical history writing that actions could be caused by human intention independent of divine causality. In stories in the book of Joshua about the emergence of Israel and Judah on the land, the primary paradigm for the process is expressed as a conquest narrative that insists that the existing populations were supposed to be annihilated according to the strict

11. "Babylonian and Assyrian Historical Texts," trans. A. Leo Oppenheim, in *Ancient Near Eastern Texts Relating to the Old Testament*, ed. James B. Pritchard, 3rd ed. (Princeton: Princeton University Press, 1969), 289.

12. "The Inscription of King Mesha," ed. K. A. D. Smelik, in Hallo, *Context of Scripture*, 2:137.

will of God because of these populations' abhorrent religious practices. However, the way the stories are written shows that some of the peoples were able by their own astuteness to circumvent their supposedly divinely justified, inevitable, and deadly fate. For example, in Joshua 2, Rahab, a prostitute in the Canaanite city-state of Jericho, cleverly convinces the Israelite spies who have come to her house to spare her and her family in the coming warfare: "Now then, since I have dealt kindly with you, swear to me by the LORD that you in turn will deal kindly with my family. Give me a sign of good faith that you will spare my father and mother, my brothers and sisters, and all who belong to them, and deliver our lives from death" (Josh. 2:12–13). This circumvention of the presumably unalterable death sentence by astute human action is reported straightforwardly, without expression of divine disapproval for what would be an evasion of God's will as the primary paradigm understood it.

The application of divine consequences for human actions that we identified as virtually inevitable in Chronicles is much looser in the books of Ezra and Nehemiah, so that events are more likely to be attributed to human will and intention. These books certainly ascribe the overall responsibility for the struggling postexilic community's future to God's care. However, a precise equation of negative consequences for bad behavior is absent, so that opposition to the postexilic community is not described as punishment for the community's lack of proper dedication or cultic purity.[13] In several stories of adversarial conflicts over the rebuilding of the temple and the city walls in Ezra and Nehemiah, the actions of Judah's enemies are described simply as human resistance, not divine punishment. For example, "But when Sanballat and Tobiah and the Arabs and the Ammonites and the Ashdodites heard that the repairing of the walls of Jerusalem was going forward and the gaps were beginning to be closed, they were very angry, and all plotted together to come and fight against Jerusalem and to cause confusion in it" (Neh. 4:7–8). Likewise, the solutions that the community comes up with for the problems caused by their adversaries are the result of

13. See Japhet, "Postexilic Historiography," 151.

human ingenuity, not specifically accredited to divine intervention. Nehemiah and the leaders devise a work plan that installs guards alongside the workers on the wall. "From that day on, half of my servants worked on construction, and half held the spears, shields, bows, and body-armor; and the leaders posted themselves behind the whole house of Judah, who were building the wall. The burden bearers carried their loads in such a way that each labored on the work with one hand and with the other held a weapon" (4:16–17).

In the historical writing of some other societies of the ancient Near East, we also find expressions of human intention free of divine determination. In the Hittite Ten Year Annals, early antagonism to the enthronement of Muršili II from enemy lands (quoted above) is expressed not as divine opposition but as the workings of merely human political motivations, in which the enemies figure that the new king, just a child, could not possibly hold on to the kingdom.[14] Another example comes from the Assyrian description of the siege of Jerusalem by Sennacherib in 701, in which the siege ends when King Hezekiah capitulates and sends payment of tribute. Hezekiah's action is attributed to a completely human reaction, when Sennacherib, through the scribes who wrote the inscription, says: "He, Hezekiah, was overwhelmed by the awesome splendor of my lordship, and he sent me [tribute consisting of] . . . his elite troops . . . with 30 talents of gold, 800 talents of silver . . . ."[15] All these ways that ancient history writing provides causal explanations of events are part of the ways the texts shape history so that it is an account that conveys understandings of divine and human agency in the events of the past.

Shaping the Story of the Past: Evaluations and Interpretations

In this section, we deal with the next two ways that ancient history writing helped to shape the story of the past so that it became more

14. "Ten Year Annals," 2:82.
15. "Sennacherib's Siege of Jerusalem," ed. Mordechai Cogan, in Hallo, *Context of Scripture*, 2:303.

than a list of dates and people. Both by providing evaluations of people and events and by providing interpretations of the meaning of the accounts related, ancient texts established ways of recalling the past so that it made sense rather than just being a random collection of memories. You may recall in hearing family stories about your ancestors that a family historian expresses opinions about the wisdom, or lack thereof, of one or more decisions made by an ancestor. Or the family storyteller might include a reflection on what a particular event means. Both evaluation and interpretation are similar approaches for reflecting on the past that are used by the ancient writers as well.

In chapter 3, we examined several techniques by which biblical historical texts report on evaluations of characters and actions. Judgments, ideals, and values are not inherent in a list of events as such; rather, they are incorporated in the way the past is related so that the interests of the text come through. While character development itself is a narrative method for implicit evaluation, the techniques of direct evaluation, repetition, patterns, and models for comparing characters all explicitly help show the interests of the texts by conveying evaluations. You will remember that one prominent evaluative standard by which characters are judged is whether they, through their actions and words, show how they stand "in the sight of the LORD." The willingness to evaluate kings and dynasties is evident in the Deuteronomistic History's consistent negative judgments about the northern state, Israel. In general, values by which people are judged in the various texts of the Deuteronomistic History and Chronicles, for example, include being loyal and committed to the Lord, keeping God's commandments, being like David in faithfulness, descending from an established and pure family lineage, and committing to the pure and proper worship of God.

History writing in other ancient cultures likewise engaged in evaluative and interpretive judgments in relating the past. Because so many of the surviving inscriptions in nations like Assyria, Hatti, Egypt, and Moab were created in the service of the ruling dynasty and its power arrangements, the interests supported in the texts

Perspectives and Interests in Modern History Writing

The assassination of President John F. Kennedy is an event now famous for the wide variety of perspectives used to tell the account. Below is a sampling of various perspectives.

A brief account from the JFK Library website:

Shortly after noon on November 22, 1963, President John F. Kennedy was assassinated as he rode in a motorcade . . . in downtown Dallas, Texas.[a]

An account that describes the controversies:

The Warren Commission's "report failed to silence conspiracy theories surrounding the event . . . and the House Select Committee concluded . . . that Kennedy was 'probably assassinated as a result of a conspiracy. . . .' The committee's findings, as with those of the Warren Commission, continue to be widely disputed."[b]

An account from a website that focuses on conspiracy theories:

There is now abundant evidence of cover-up taking place at the highest levels of government after the assassination. Furthermore, and even more disturbingly, the best leads to the nature of the murder conspiracy itself point in the direction of U.S. intelligence agencies and the U.S. military.[c]

From an account about Kennedy's Secret Service agents:

The interviews with the agents "offer a new window into an event that transformed not just the nation, but also the men who were supposed to keep him safe."[d]

From an article written almost fifty years after the assassination:

The time for conspiracy theories has passed and the time for accountability is coming. . . . Allegations [from a Cuban specialist at the CIA] advertently highlight a truth that the CIA and my friends in the Washington press corps prefer not to acknowledge: There is a lot more evidence of CIA negligence in JFK's assassination than Cuban complicity.[e]

a. "November 22, 1963: Death of the President," *John F. Kennedy Presidential Library & Museum*, accessed December 31, 2012, http://www.jfklibrary.org/JFK/JFK-in-History/November-22-1963-Death-of-the-President.aspx.
b. "Nov 22, 1963: John F. Kennedy Assassinated," *History.com*, accessed December 31, 2012, http://www.history.com/this-day-in-history/john-f-kennedy-assassinated.
c. Rex Bradford, "The JFK Assassination," *History Matters*, accessed December 31, 2012, http://www.history-matters.com/jfkmurder.htm.
d. "JFK Requested Bodyguards to Back Off," *Discovery News*, last updated February 11, 2013, http://news.discovery.com/history/jfk-assassination-secret-service.html.
e. Jefferson Morley, "What Can We Do about JFK's Murder?," *The Atlantic*, November 21, 2012, http://www.theatlantic.com/national/archive/2012/11/what-can-we-do-about-jfks-murder/265520/.

through evaluation and interpretation likewise serve those interests. Nonetheless, examples show how these societies shaped the
past in their historiography. For example, the Weidner Chronicle,
an Assyrian inscription that may predate the time period we are
focusing on, gives accounts of various kings and assesses each one
on whether he honored or damaged the cult of the god Marduk,
paralleling how the Deuteronomistic History judges kings on their
fidelity to God.[16] Also, the Apology of Esarhaddon, already cited,
defends the kingship of this ruler against any opposition by recounting both how the gods favored his rule and how he won out
against his brothers, who were rivals for the throne. The inscription
evaluates the brothers' behavior as evil, using a phrase that should
be familiar by now.

> (When) the real meaning (of this act) [his enthronement] dawned
> upon my brothers, they abandoned godliness, put their trust in bold
> actions, planning an evil plot. . . . Thereupon, my brothers went out
> of their senses, doing everything that is wicked in (the eyes of) the
> gods and mankind, and (continued) their evil machinations.[17]

A final example comes from a text from the Persian Empire,
which ruled over the ancient Near East, including Judah, from 539
to 333 BCE. The Cyrus Cylinder supports the legitimacy of Cyrus,
the king who conquered Babylon and brought the Persians to control
over an extended empire, first by evaluating the previous ruler of
Babylon as unworthy because of his failures in the religious sphere:
"[The correct images of the gods he removed from their thrones]
. . . daily he did blabber [incorrect prayers]. . . . The worship of
Marduk, the king of gods, he [chang]ed into abomination."[18] As
this inscription relates the history of the establishment of the Persian Empire, Cyrus's overthrow of Babylon is an act decreed by
the gods because he was a "righteous ruler" who would treat the
gods properly. Thus the negative judgment against the failures of

16. Dijkstra, "'As for the Other Events,'" 35.
17. "Babylonian and Assyrian Historical Texts," 289.
18. Ibid., 315 (brackets original).

the previous ruler helps shape the interpretation of the event of the overthrow as a divinely directed event.

In all these examples from the historical writing of this era, both in the Bible and in other texts, we see that evaluation and interpretation go hand in hand with all the other techniques we have examined that are used in creating accounts of the past. When a text uses this wide variety of techniques to communicate its interests, it is thereby creating an interpretation of the past. The evaluative elements demonstrate this more clearly than do other, more subtle effects. However, narrative methods like characterization and detail, selection of sources, creation of patterns, and explanations of causality all work together to shape how the text conveys what is important to know about the past. We have seen how a text like Chronicles interprets the whole course of events in Judah through its clear concentration on David and his role in establishing a righteous dynasty and well-ordered worship. We have seen how an Assyrian text like the Apology of Esarhaddon interprets the past in order to support the legitimacy of the king. These are but two examples of interpretive approaches in the illustrations we have been using throughout this examination.

That these ancient texts were shaped to present an interpretation of the past by communicating particular interests should be well established by now. What is even more interesting is that in the literatures of these ancient societies, including Israel and Judah, there are examples of differing interpretations being preserved even within the texts associated with one ruler or dynasty. While it is apparent that almost all ancient texts produced by the scribes of the various royal houses have some sense of the proper way to interpret the past, in a few cases we have enough distinct surviving texts to see some development and variation in how the past was recounted. Of course, where two different nations remember the same event in the past, we would expect each to present its own interpretation of that event. However, we can also see some differentiation in interpretation within a group of texts from one ruler's reign.

For example, one historian of the Assyrian Empire has studied a series of inscriptions about Shalmaneser III's battle in 853 BCE against a coalition of western kings, including Israel, that come from a varying number of years after the event.[19] While most scholars think that the battle actually was not a victory for the Assyrians, the way the battle is related in the series of inscriptions changes over time—for example, the number of dead killed by the Assyrians is inflated as the years go on, and thus the "victory" appears more certain.[20] Such differences in how that past event is related did, of course, serve the purposes of the ruling house but show that an idea once put in stone was not always "set in stone."

A second example also comes from Assyria, from a document named the Babylon Inscription from the time of Esarhaddon (680–669 BCE), which describes the Assyrian king's building projects in the city of Babylon.[21] A detailed study shows that the preserved manuscripts, which number over a dozen, are by no means exact copies but rather show a number of variations through several different versions in the way the episodes of the account are related. Overall the versions tell of the fate of the city and its cult centers, through floods, neglect, and outright destruction, and then rebuilding. The versions almost always use the particularly Babylonian religious understanding that the gods' will was enacted and could be known through astronomical observations and omens. For example, concerning whether Esarhaddon should rebuild a temple, most of the versions say something like this: "In the bowl of the diviners, trustworthy oracles were set for me. Concerning the reconstruction of Babylon and the restoration of the temple . . . I trusted their true 'yes.'"[22] But one version entirely omits all references to omens and astronomy and interprets the same events as the other versions relate, but without the Babylonian religious point of view.[23] The scholar who studied these differences in the particular version notes that the distinctive interpretation was a deliberate variation in ideology

19. Younger, "Neo-Assyrian and Israelite History," 247.
20. Ibid., 255.
21. Mordechai Cogan, "Omens and Ideology in the Babylon Inscription of Esarhaddon," in Tadmor and Weinfeld, *History, Historiography and Interpretation*, 76.
22. Ibid., 79.
23. Ibid., 80.

by the scribes who created this inscription, suggesting differences among the scribes who produced the copies. "[The variations] were found to be expressions of a distinct ideological point of view in the debate over Babylon at Esarhaddon's court. . . . Many groups vied for the king's ear; their ideological platforms were presented in literary compositions, such as the Babylonian Inscription."[24]

When it comes to biblical historiography, differences in interpretation should already be familiar to you—we have noted in several ways how the books of Chronicles present a different interpretation of the meaning of the events of the Davidic dynasty than does the Deuteronomistic History. Of course, the principal outlines of these theological presentations reflect similar values, such as their fidelity to the Lord, their focus on Judah and Jerusalem, and their interest in the incidents surrounding kingship and the temple. However, as we have seen, there are distinctions between how these two histories interpret the past, according to the particular theological focus of the texts. For example, the Deuteronomistic History presents Solomon as the king who was in charge of designing and building the temple. Chronicles, with its glorification of David, attributes all the design details to David, who had the entire temple planned out before his death; Solomon merely enacted David's plans.

Another example of different interpretations of the past between books comes from a comparison of Ezra and Nehemiah with Chronicles, particularly on the issue of the inclusion of foreigners in the postexilic community. Ezra and Nehemiah consistently define the community of "Israel" to include only priests, Levites, and those Jews who returned from exile to Judah. The interests of these books to provide strong boundaries for the identity of the community mean that even Jews who had remained in the land of Judah during the exile were not really included in the interests of the text.[25] The books of Chronicles, through the use of genealogies and stories about the reestablishment of postexilic Jerusalem, image a more inclusive community. Here included groups incorporate resident aliens and

24. Ibid., 84.
25. Japhet, "Postexilic Historiography," 158.

foreigners, and in particular the Jews who had remained in the land.
For example, see this inclusive description of the community that
is reported to have been in attendance at the Passover celebration
by Hezekiah many years previously—a community description that
provides a model for the postexilic boundaries: "The whole assembly
of Judah, the priests and the Levites, and the whole assembly that
came out of Israel, and the resident aliens who came out of the
land of Israel, and the resident aliens who lived in Judah, rejoiced"
(2 Chron. 30:25).

In the differences between Ezra and Nehemiah and the books of
Chronicles, these varying interpretations of the boundaries of the
community are communicated through how the texts write about
the past. While it is beyond the scope of our study to imagine why
or how various interpretations of the past come to be included in
different accounts, it is likely that the various interpretations correspond to theological differences among groups in the postexilic
community itself. And, in any case, the various interests each text
conveys have something to say to the audiences of the texts, a matter
to which we will return in the next section.

It is possible also to note variations in interpretation of past events
within adjacent books or within a single book, a more particular
case of accounts of the past that communicate a variety of interests.
Two examples from the Deuteronomistic History can demonstrate
diversity in how an aspect of the past is presented—the emergence
of Israel on the land and the establishment of the monarchy. First,
as we noted above, the emergence of the tribes of Israel and Judah
on the land in the book of Joshua presents a principal paradigm
of a total conquest by a united military force of twelve tribes. The
accounts contained in this story line communicate strong theological
interests in defense of a united tribal community that overcomes
foreign peoples and their gods. These summary verses are characteristic of this way of relating the past:

> So Joshua took all that land: the hill country and all the Negeb and
> all the land of Goshen and the lowland and the Arabah and the hill
> country of Israel and its lowland, from Mount Halak, which rises

toward Seir, as far as Baal-gad in the valley of Lebanon below Mount
Hermon. He took all their kings, struck them down, and put them to
death. . . . So Joshua took the whole land, according to all that the
LORD had spoken to Moses; and Joshua gave it for an inheritance
to Israel according to their tribal allotments. And the land had rest
from war. (Josh. 11:16–17, 23)

However, a diverse view of how the tribes emerged on the land is
communicated in other texts, in particular in the book of Judges.
In these accounts, more of the original peoples of the land survive
to be included in the emerging community, and there are tensions
among the tribal groups of Israel and Judah themselves. A more
varied account of the whole process is communicated, as the following text illustrates:

The LORD was with Judah, and he took possession of the hill country,
but could not drive out the inhabitants of the plain, because they
had chariots of iron. . . . But the Benjaminites did not drive out the
Jebusites who lived in Jerusalem; so the Jebusites have lived in Jerusalem among the Benjaminites to this day. . . . Manasseh did not
drive out the inhabitants of Beth-shean and its villages, or Taanach
and its villages, or the inhabitants of Dor and its villages, or the
inhabitants of Ibleam and its villages, or the inhabitants of Megiddo
and its villages; but the Canaanites continued to live in that land.
When Israel grew strong, they put the Canaanites to forced labor,
but did not in fact drive them out. And Ephraim did not drive out
the Canaanites who lived in Gezer; but the Canaanites lived among
them in Gezer. (Judg. 1:19, 21, 27–29)

These variations in how the past is interpreted are interwoven in the
texts of Joshua and Judges, which seems to indicate a historiography
that can live with a certain amount of inconsistency. However, the
overall account still communicates a theological conclusion—namely,
that under God's direction and guidance the tribes of Israel and
Judah inhabited the land, even if by a variety of means.

Our second example shows variation in how the past is presented
within a single book. The establishment of the monarchy as the form

of government for the states of Israel and Judah is a central interest of the Deuteronomistic History. However, the story of how this process happened also shows diverse interpretations as that era of the past is related in the book of 1 Samuel. What comes across in the text is that differing views are possible about the costs and benefits of monarchy as the account relates the process by which tribal leadership moved toward a more centralized form of governance under a king. One view the story communicates is that kingship was a form of governance explicitly installed by God that will bring blessings for the people. Some of the texts about the anointing of Saul as the first king illustrate this theological interpretation of kingship.

> Now the day before Saul came, the Lord had revealed to Samuel: "Tomorrow about this time I will send to you a man from the land of Benjamin, and you shall anoint him to be ruler over my people Israel. He shall save my people from the hand of the Philistines; for I have seen the suffering of my people, because their outcry has come to me." (1 Sam. 9:15–16)

> So all the people went to Gilgal, and there they made Saul king before the Lord in Gilgal. There they sacrificed offerings of well-being before the Lord, and there Saul and all the Israelites rejoiced greatly. (1 Sam. 11:15)

A very different interpretation of kingship as an institution is communicated in a nearby chapter of 1 Samuel. As we saw in chapter 1 above, a monarchical form of government in an agrarian society gives a lot of power to an elite class, power that the elite typically use for their own purposes. This understanding of kingship is presented in the following passage (note that we used this same passage to illustrate the use of repetition in chap. 3):

> But the thing displeased Samuel when [the elders of Israel] said, "Give us a king to govern us." Samuel prayed to the Lord, and the Lord said to Samuel, "Listen to the voice of the people in all that they say to you; for they have not rejected you, but they have rejected me from being king over them. . . . Only—you shall solemnly warn

them, and show them the ways of the king who shall reign over them." So Samuel reported all the words of the LORD to the people who were asking him for a king. He said, "These will be the ways of the king who will reign over you: he will take your sons and appoint them to his chariots and to be his horsemen . . . and some to plow his ground and to reap his harvest. . . . He will take your daughters to be perfumers and cooks and bakers. He will take the best of your fields and vineyards and olive orchards and give them to his courtiers. He will take one-tenth of your grain and of your vineyards and give it to his officers and his courtiers. . . . And in that day you will cry out because of your king, whom you have chosen for yourselves; but the LORD will not answer you in that day." (1 Sam. 8:6–7, 9–15, 18)

While maintaining the representations of both points of view, these chapters in 1 Samuel also convey a compromise about kingship—that no matter how much power the king has, he must obey the command-ments of God. The story relates how Samuel phrases this in his farewell address: "If you will fear the LORD and serve him and heed his voice and not rebel against the commandment of the LORD, and if both you and the king who reigns over you will follow the LORD your God, it will be well" (1 Sam. 12:14). One scholar phrases well the ambiguity of interpretation about kingship conveyed in 1 Samuel and in the follow-ing story of the monarchy in the rest of the Deuteronomistic History:

> This same ambiguity surfaces in Dtr's [the writer of the Deuterono-mistic History] retrospect on the monarchy as a whole: kings caused Israel and Judah a great deal of trouble, but they also brought some rewards. . . . Thus, Dtr may be suspicious of monarchy, but he does not see it as evil. After all, 1 Samuel 8–12 ends with YHWH endorsing monarchy provided that the king and his subjects remain faithful. This faithfulness to YHWH is Dtr's primary concern.[26]

That the account in 1 Samuel includes both interpretations of mon-archy as an institution conveys that debate and dialogue are possible about such topics in the theological interests of the texts.

26. Steven McKenzie, "The Trouble with Kingship," in Pury et al., *Israel Constructs Its History*, 308.

Shaping the Story of the Past: Addressing the Present

We have just studied a number of approaches that ancient texts use to shape the story of the past: they provide descriptions of patterns perceived in past events, explanations of causes, evaluation of events and persons, and interpretations of the past. These approaches reinforce and complement the extended study we did in chapter 3 about how biblical history writing conveys its interests. The final aspect of the shaping of the past that we will explore builds on all this analysis of the interests conveyed in ancient history writing. What becomes apparent is that ancient texts often appear to use the interests they express to address the needs and concerns of the time of the document or inscription, rather than to tell about the past for the sake of a neutral record or for the sake of the past itself. That is, ancient history writing seems to be shaped in order to be useful for the time period of the creator of a text or of the institution that directed the writing of the text, like a royal dynasty or administration. You may have seen this kind of approach in memories from grandparents who want to help a younger generation learn from the elder's own experiences. Or family historians researching ancestors may have a genuine interest in the past, but they may come to realize that they are also learning about their own identities. Further, they might, through the family history they write, include insights useful for their contemporary family members that they learned from their study of the past.

Two determinations combine in coming to an assessment of how and whether an ancient document addressed its own ancient "present moment." The first determination is done by examining the texts themselves to reveal the interests of the texts, a topic already well illustrated. But the second determination relies on placing those interests into a time period or situation that seems a reasonable social location for the text. Sometimes a text can be located with some precision if it contains a date; in other cases, the time of the text must be ascertained through context, language, and so on, and may be only an approximate date. In coming to a judgment about whether the interests expressed by the texts might fit into a particular situation, scholars are making a historical assessment about how an inscription or document might have been used in its time. For all the historical writing in the ancient societies that we have been examining, scholars voice considered opinions about what contexts and situations ancient texts addressed. And in particular, while the concern of this book is not to deal with historical events and situations from the biblical record, we will consider the work of scholars who describe the time periods and situations addressed by the interests of the historical books. Our intention is not to prove exactly what the biblical historians intended by their writing but rather to indicate how the interests expressed in the biblical historical books might fit and address probable ancient contexts.

In some cases of inscriptions and documents from Assyria or Hatti, the interests expressed by the shaping of the past clearly address a particular time period or situation. For example, in the Plague Prayers by the Hittite king Muršili (cited above), the prayers clearly relate past events as a part of a prayer and plea by the king to the gods for help during an extended plague. Another Hittite document, the Proclamation of Telipinu, is a political document that establishes rules for succession of kings and recites the past to justify the issuance of such rules.[27] In other cases, it appears that inscriptions that shaped accounts of past military campaigns and royal building projects could be useful for a dynasty or ruler in the ancient world. The many inscriptions placed on monuments along the roadways and in cities of countries conquered by an empire like Assyria helped the kings enforce their domination and control. The past recounted in the inscription of the many victories (whether actual victories or not!) and monumental building projects conveyed the idea that it would be a bad move to resist the empire. You might remember a famous line from *Star Trek*, where an alien empire, the Borg, confronts *Enterprise* captain Jean-Luc Picard to intimidate him: "Resistance is futile." Further, a document like the Apology

---

27. "The Proclamation of Telipinu," ed. Th. P. J. van den Hout, in *The Context of Scripture*, ed. William Hallo, vol. 1, *Canonical Compositions from the Biblical World* (Leiden: Brill, 1997), 194.

of Esarhaddon communicates interests that legitimate the rule of the king against other contenders and in turn helps establish the rightful succession of Esarhaddon's own son when the time comes.[28]

The interests conveyed by biblical historical writing also are considered by scholars to address the needs and concerns of the times in which they were written and/or edited and rewritten. While there are ongoing debates about the dating of the various editions of the Deuteronomistic History, and about the process of composition for books like Ezra and Nehemiah, the idea that the historical writing in these books addresses in some way the era of the writing is well established. In the biblical historical books, there even are indications that the texts are aware that they use the past to address and appeal to the present. Throughout these books, but especially in the Deuteronomistic History, the phrase "to this day" is added at the end of numerous accounts when the text wants to point out that a custom, name, or location is still relevant. The phrase is used several times each in the books of Chronicles, Ezra, and Nehemiah, and more pointedly, it is used over forty times in the books of the Deuteronomistic History and is a persistent part of the way these texts present the current relevance of the past. One example comes from the description of the ark of the covenant when it was brought into the original temple in Jerusalem during Solomon's reign, in verses that are virtually identical in both 1 Kings 8 and 2 Chronicles 5.

> Then the priests brought the ark of the covenant of the LORD to its place, in the inner sanctuary of the house, in the most holy place, underneath the wings of the cherubim. . . . The poles were so long that the ends of the poles were seen from the holy place in front of the inner sanctuary; but they could not be seen from outside; they are there to this day. (2 Chron. 5:7, 9)

What is interesting is that both Chronicles and the final edition of the Deuteronomistic History were finalized in the postexilic period, when the original temple had been destroyed, and it is unlikely that the original poles for carrying the ark actually could have been seen

---

28. Tadmor, "Autobiographical Apology," 54.

"to this day." However, both texts keep that image alive in how they are written; such a clear interest expressed in the texts may have served to validate the origins of the inner sanctuary in the rebuilt temple of the postexilic period.

In fact, when scholars consider the situations probably addressed by the interests of the biblical historical writings, the needs and concerns of the exilic and postexilic community are foremost because it is in those circumstances that the writing of the books was finalized. To illustrate how the shaping of the various historical books we have considered met the needs and concerns of that period, we will give a selection of judgments from scholars. One scholar, referring to the possibility that the Deuteronomistic History underwent one edition before the exile and a second edition during the exile, phrases the theological concerns of the history writing in this way:

> Deuteronomistic theology is, then, an explicit ideology developed in response to the conditions of late-seventh-century and early-sixth-century Judah, as a means by which the newly emerging Israel, the people of Yahweh, might identify itself, both for itself and for others, articulating its goals and justifying them through an account of how it related to others and how it overcame its own internal conflicts.[29]

Another scholar describes more directly how the writing of an account of the past in the Deuteronomistic History itself was meant to address the needs of the exilic and postexilic community. Even though the Deuteronomistic History ends with the destruction of Jerusalem (2 Kings 25) seen as divine judgment for the actions of the people, the interests of the text help convey that there is meaning in the disaster by looking back at the history of the nation.

> The Dtr author has faith in the "logic in history." This means that history is not marked by a profound absurdity, but that it is—in a certain perspective—completely reasonable ("logical"). . . . The

29. Andrew D. H. Mayes, "Deuteronomistic Ideology and the Theology of the Old Testament," in Pury et al., *Israel Constructs Its History*, 472.

"logic in history" was particularly important for the people in the Babylonian exile: a *meaning* had to be given to the national disaster. For a profoundly human life, it is not enough to survive a catastrophe physically, but it is necessary to give a meaning to what one has experienced.[30]

It is likewise possible to give examples of how scholars think the books of Chronicles, Ezra, and Nehemiah address their "present" day through the interests they communicate in the shaping of history. All these books were written in the postexilic period when the newly reestablished community was in various stages of consolidating its institutions, identity, and boundaries. The books of Chronicles, which retell the story of the Davidic monarchy, use that history writing for very contemporary needs.

> [The Chronicler's] major motive is legitimization, based on the concept of "genealogy." Present day institutions are legitimized by the uncovering of their origins. The "writing of David" or the "order of the king," which were inspired and sanctified by God or "the command of the prophets," are the source of authority from which contemporary institutions and concepts receive their validity.[31]

This same scholar has considered the historiography of Ezra and Nehemiah, and how they share views through their shaping of history, "which is the spiritual response to an actual historical reality."[32] The scholar goes on to describe the situation these books address. "There was now a rooted and active community, with a temple whose arrangements were being consolidated and a lifestyle that had as its center the worship of the Lord. This present situation, under the auspices and benevolence of the Persian kings, is conceived in Ezra-Nehemiah as governed by God's providence."[33]

30. Martin Rose, "Deuteronomistic Ideology and Theology of the Old Testament," in Pury et al., *Israel Constructs Its History*, 447.
31. Japhet, "Postexilic Historiography," 165. The term *the Chronicler* refers to the author of the books of Chronicles.
32. Ibid., 155.
33. Ibid., 157.

However, in their history writing, Ezra and Nehemiah show interest only in aspects of the past that will address present needs. For example, the strict boundaries of the community mean that "the most fundamental issues of identity and continuity" are traced back to the limited past of the people "of the 'exile,' the people from Judah, Benjamin, and Levi, who came from Babylon to settle in Judah,"[34] not to other scattered tribes or Jews dispersed in other lands. In ways like these, the various historical books we have considered use their shaping of accounts and the interests they convey to address the situations in which they were written, even as they recount the past.

Conclusion

We have used these final two chapters of the book to explore the characteristics of biblical history writing that mark its particular way of doing history. We have shown examples from the biblical texts as well as numerous parallel examples from other history writing contemporaneous with the Bible. We made and illustrated the point that while ancient history writing does not use the same standards of critical evaluation of sources and balanced judgment as modern history writing, it nonetheless has standards and practices that make it actual writing about the past. Understanding biblical history writing on its own terms will help you appreciate how the biblical texts do indeed tell the story of the past. Our final task will be to gather up all the characteristics of biblical history writing that we have examined in this volume in order to create a working definition of biblical historiography. That will serve as a summary and overview of our work, and to that we turn in the conclusion.

Suggested Reading

See the list at the end of chapter 4.

34. Ibid., 157–58.

Discussion Questions

1. Think of ways that modern writers of documents like history books, speeches, blogs, and emails shape their writing so that it conveys their intentions. How do these types of shaping compare with those used in ancient history writing?

2. Compare a parallel story from 1 Kings and 2 Chronicles, the story of King Jehoshaphat of Judah in 1 Kings 22:41–50 and 2 Chronicles 17:1–19. How are these portraits different? What types of evaluative judgments are used in each story? How does causality work in each story?

3. What types of modern writing are used to address concerns contemporary with the writer's time? Take a look at some newspaper editorials or op-ed pieces, blog postings, or websites where the writers are trying to address a contemporary issue. How do these compare to biblical history writing?

Conclusion

Toward a Definition of Biblical Historiography

The study we have undertaken in this volume was aimed at answering some basic questions about the history writing or historiography in the Old Testament. Our questions were these: How do we read the historical books in the Old Testament well? What do we need to know about this part of Scripture in order to appreciate the beauty and meanings of the text? We approached these questions by also asking: What is this document? Why is it written this way? What else do we need to know to understand it well? Through a variety of approaches to the biblical historical books, we have developed some answers to these questions. We first considered the background of biblical historiography, looking at the context of the books and the time period in which they were written. Here we considered the larger world in and behind the texts, using knowledge gained from approaches like sociology, geography, archaeology, and ancient history.

When we turned to examining the content and format of the biblical historical books, we first considered the narrative style and artistry of biblical history writing, highlighting the kinds of storytelling techniques used by the ancient writers to shape the narratives they told. In the third chapter, we examined how the narratives also convincingly convey evaluations, values, opinions, and worldviews. Seeing how the texts communicate these interests shows that they are highly shaped, convincing theological documents that work as persuasive writing to convey the thought world of the text. Finally, in the last two chapters, we examined the methods and conventions by which these books transmit their account of the past. By referring to the methods of ancient history writing in many examples from other ancient societies, we have been able to see how the texts recount stories about events, people, and places of their own eras with seriousness and respect in order to bring out the meaning of the past for their ancient audiences.

If we bring together what we have observed in these chapters, we can propose the following definition of biblical historiography:

Biblical history writing constructed an account of the past that reflected the contexts of its world as the background for its writing and that

- wrote in a narrative format that recounted tales about past events, people, and places, using the techniques of narrative art;
- conveyed a range of interests through persuasive techniques by which the text was shaped;
- employed techniques to recount the past, including

    using a chronological structure to organize the flow of the narrative,

    incorporating sources from previous oral traditions and written traditions, and

    shaping the story of the past through methods like selectivity and provision of explanations and evaluations; and

- addressed the needs and concerns of the audience of the document to make the past meaningful.

To provide a summary that shows how our examination in the previous chapters supports this definition of biblical history writing, we will gather the details of our study in clear visual formats.

These can serve as summary lists to which you can refer when you study texts from the biblical historical books.

Writing in a Narrative Format

The first element of the style of biblical historical writing is its narrative format. Here is a list of the questions we developed for studying the narrative artistry of biblical history writing.

Plot Development: Beginnings and Endings

Where are the beginning and end of the narrative? How are these marked?

Is the narrative part of a larger story or ongoing story line?

Plot Development: Scenic Structure

What events/scenes take place? Who is in each scene?

What are the transitions between scenes?

Plot Development: Story Arc

What is the problem or conflict driving the plot?

What complications are introduced as the plot is worked out?

Where is the crisis or turning point (or points)?

What happens in the resolution phase?

Are expectations that are set up by the story fulfilled, broken, changed?

Plot Development: Sequences

Does repetition occur at any level within the story—words, phrases, events, scenes?

Are there any "command-enactment-report" sequences or "forecast-enactment-report" sequences in the narrative?

If so, does the repeated element repeat, confirm, change, contradict, or comment on the previous speech/event/element?

Characterization: Direct Description

What direct description of characters is given by the narrator?

Characterization: By Actions

How do actions by characters aid in their characterization?
Do the actions give a depiction of the type of person?

Characterization: By Dialogue

How does dialogue add to the characterization of the main
characters?
Who speaks in the story? Who does not speak?
Are a character's words reliable, confirmed by others, by the narrator, by events?

Point of View

Through whose eyes are we seeing each scene?
Within an all-knowing narrator's viewpoint, do we see any other
points of view?
Do we hear the inner thoughts of any character?
Is the point of view of any character consistently denied to the
reader?

Time Flow

How are events related in the sequencing of the story?
Are there indications of simultaneous events, use of the past, or
indications of the future?
Where does time move slowly or quickly in the story?
Does time jump in transitions between scenes?

Conveying a Range of Interests

Our next element of definition is that biblical historical texts convey a range of interests in such things as the values and evaluations they persuasively communicate. To summarize the examination of the techniques by which textual interests are communicated, here is a list of the persuasive methods that we covered.

Presence

What words, phrases, and ideas are brought forward by the ways the text makes them present to the reader?

What is emphasized by the text or across texts, particularly as repetition keeps coming back to words, phrases, and ideas?

Authority

What characters have authority in the story, or in what ways are certain figures made the focus of authority arguments so that they function with influence in subsequent chapters?

How do characters then use their authority to affect or shape the actions and ideas of others?

Repetition

How is repetition used to craft a persuasive argument or make a point or idea more evident and forceful in the text?

Where do you see repetition working across adjacent texts, and where does it work across lengthy spans of chapters?

Analogies between Accounts

What analogies are created between accounts, in which two figures or events are shaped so that they resonate with each other and thus inform the reader about the characteristics of both ends of the analogy?

Direct Evaluation

What direct evaluation is included in the text?

How is it expressed, and what values, judgments, and ideals does it convey?

Patterns

What patterns are set up in the text and, in particular, across texts? What are the elements of the pattern in each case?

How do direct evaluation and pattern setting work together to convey judgments across stories?

What does the omission of an established pattern communicate about a figure, event, or idea?

Models

What figures are set up as models for other characters in the historical books?

What values and ideas does the model express, and how do those values and ideas transfer to the other figures who follow the model?

Dramatic Impact

How does the story create dramatic impact through strong words, dramatic language, vivid scenes, and powerful characters?

What does the dramatic impact tell you about where the story focuses its interests?

Details

What details are included in the text?

Where does the flow of the story in the text slow down to include extra attention to particulars, including formats like lists and extended description?

While doing our study of the techniques of persuasive writing, we examined numerous texts from the historical books. This work showed that we could create a summary of the various interests that have emerged in our review of biblical historiography. The list below accumulates ideas across the range of examples we used and provides a brief summary of the commitments and viewpoints of the historical books. You can see that it is fair to label these interests "theological" in that they all have to do with one or more of the following questions: What is God's nature? What is human nature? How are humans to relate to God and to one another?

1. The Lord is the ultimate authority in the story of the biblical historical books. God makes divine will known through various messengers and leaders who are thus also endowed with authority. Prophets in particular are authoritative messengers of the Lord who bring to humans God's word not only about human behavior and ethical standards but also about God's power, compassion, and care for the most vulnerable.

2. David is a model of exemplary behavior as a king and man of God who also serves as a model for judging other kings and leaders.

3. Authority is vested in other leaders in the biblical historical books, and new leaders are reminded of the values they should embody in leading God's people. Sometimes authority is seen in surprising figures who would normally not have been rated in the ancient context as wielding legitimate power, such as women and enemies.

4. Kings as authority figures in the Deuteronomistic History are reminded about and evaluated on how their abilities and actions measure up "in the sight of the Lord." Kings are capable of both ethical behavior and ruthless actions. Values by which they are judged include loyalty to the Lord, keeping commandments, being strong and courageous, and remembering their connection to God as the source of their power. In the Deuteronomistic History, David acts as a model because

"his heart was true to the Lord" and he was remembered as keeping the commandments of God, particularly in keeping proper rituals for worship of God and God alone.

5. Leaders like Ezra and Nehemiah in the postexilic period are exemplary as they show care for the values associated with rebuilding the temple, propagating the law, supporting the priesthood and proper worship, and enforcing the true boundaries, lineages, and heritage of the people. In Chronicles, Ezra, and Nehemiah, David is a model for keeping the law of Moses, but these books emphasize that he is also the originator of proper worship rituals, orders of religious personnel, and the music of the temple that the postexilic community should follow.

6. The northern kingdom of Israel existed alongside the southern kingdom of Judah for two centuries. The Deuteronomistic History books relate tales from Israel and include its kings in royal chronologies. However, the texts report that Israel, beginning with its founding king, pursued aberrant worship practices that were "evil in the sight of the Lord" and doomed its future. The books of Chronicles, which relate the same historical period, virtually ignore Israel as a separate state while making an appeal to include the tribes and lineages that made up the northern state within their focus on Judah, Jerusalem, and the Davidic monarchy.

Employing Techniques to Recount the Past

Through our step-by-step review of how history is written in the biblical books and other ancient documents, we also saw the wide range of ways that the biblical historical books told about the past. These techniques are the substance and characteristics of biblical writing when it shaped an account of the past. The techniques include the following:

Using a chronological structure to organize the flow of the narrative, in particular including phrases and formulas that create a structure of eras and regnal periods

Incorporating sources from oral traditions and written documents and making explicit references to other sources

Shaping the story of the past in order to communicate particular interests through the ways the story is conveyed, including

>   *Selecting only the particular sources* that were helpful for the story being told

>   *Offering descriptions of patterns perceived in past events* to create order and regularity rather than a recounting of random or disorganized events and to draw attention to connections among people and events

>   *Providing explanations of the causes of events and situations*, especially the ever-present assumption in ancient texts of divine causality and the intervention of God in human affairs, but also the concomitant possibility of human motivations and intentions

>   *Presenting evaluations of events and persons* that include the presentation of judgments, ideals, and values in the recounting of the past

>   *Proposing interpretations of the past* that in most cases convey a reading of the past standardized for the royal or religious origins of the texts, but that in a few cases show some development, variation, and distinctions in how the past was recounted

Using the interests expressed to address the needs and concerns of the time of the document, so that ancient history writing is shaped in order to be useful for the time period of the text

If you think back to the illustration used at the beginning of this book, of finding an old family history in your grandmother's attic, you can imagine now how full and important that history might be. Even though your grandmother (and perhaps now you) may find an emotional attachment to the story, you can also see that such a story contains and conveys much more meaning than just a simple list of dates or names. Our review of biblical history writing has demonstrated the many ways that history writing in the Bible was shaped to be a deliberate and careful theological account of the past. The intense care taken to tell about the past in particular ways shows that the biblical historical books were built on the assumption that knowing the past was important, perhaps vitally important to the life and identity of its audience. Knowing about the past addressed and showed concern for the situation of the audience and its social institutions, roles, leaders, political decisions, events, and peoples. Biblical historiography addressed its contemporaries through the fascinating stories being told, through the theological interests being communicated, and through the ways the accounts of the past were conveyed. It is clear that all these stories of the past, with their art-istry and persuasiveness, with their insistent explanations, points of view, and values, were far from a neutral, dispassionate reporting of cold, hard facts. These stories of the people and their leaders were compelling, the theological interests and commitments were important, and the past of this people with their God was worth remembering. This is the stuff of biblical history.

Discussion Question

> What aspects of biblical history writing will you want to keep in mind as you read biblical texts? Make a list of these, perhaps using the phrase "When I read a biblical historical text, I want to remember that . . ."

Scripture Index

Subject Index